TIM GOSLING

CLASSIC
THE DNA OF FURNITURE DESIGN
CONTEMPORARY

Thames & Hudson

I would like to dedicate this book to my father,
Professor Raymond Gosling (1926–2015),
who took the first photograph of the
DNA double helix.

Classic Contemporary:
The DNA of Furniture Design
© 2015 T. Gosling Ltd

Designed by Isambard Thomas

First published in 2015 in hardcover
in the United States of America by
Thames & Hudson Inc., 500 Fifth Avenue,
New York, New York 10110

thamesandhudsonusa.com

Library of Congress Catalog Card Number
2015941293

ISBN 978-0-500-51783-3

Printed and bound in China
by C&C Offset Printing Co. Ltd

[endpapers]
Detail of the pietra dura panel illustrated on
pages 36–37, showing burnt marble pieces
shaded to create the illusion of rose petals.
These were hand-cut by Pitti Mosaici
in Florence.

[pages 2–3]
A black vellum and bronze dining table
occupies the central space of a room whose
walls and cornice are wrapped in a deep
aubergine silk velvet. The fireplace is made
from solid pieces of carved Porta marble.
The pair of side tables are lacquered and inset
with bronze inlays. The chandelier is by
Hervé Van der Straeten, while the interior
design is by Todhunter Earle.

[page 6]
Detail of a Bombay rosewood and bone
plinth with solid blocks in acrylic slicing
through the design to create the illusion
that the objects on top are floating.
The plinths and dining room can be seen
in their entirety on page 205.

[page 9]
A detail of a bespoke Bramah key, made by
a lock company founded in London in 1784.
All the keys in the santos rosewood library
are embossed with the Gosling furniture
stamp. The room itself is illustrated on
pages 144–45.

Foreword

I came to know Tim through his work. We were fellow members of a committee whose role was to protect, display and enhance the art, furniture and design of the Athenaeum, one of London's finest and best-preserved buildings. Tim's comprehensive knowledge of everything to do with construction and decoration, from architecture and furniture to paintings and silverware, was not only instructive and enlightening – it was also highly infectious. Tim was a great communicator, able to mix authority and humour, expertise and enthusiasm in a way that drew us all in. I was never made to feel ignorant, even though I was; for what motivated Tim was a delight in sharing what he saw as the beauty of good work. No ivory tower for him: the place to be was out there on the rooftops, spreading the word.

The more I've got to know Tim, and to witness the lengths he will go to make his subject entertaining, the more I feel we are kindred spirits. We are both shameless performers, but also duly respectful of creativity – not as something dry or academic, but as something that binds us all, at whatever level, in participation and celebration.

This book has all the hallmarks of Tim's approach to life and art, his respect for creative expression and craftsmanship, and his delight in seeing things done well. One of its strengths is that, while Tim's own influences are acknowledged, his preferences never threaten us – partly because Tim himself is essentially open-minded, and partly because he is a good historian who wants to present the full picture and then let readers make up their own minds. He takes us on a ride through the history of design over the last three hundred years that is as informative as it is lively. He knows the importance of a dramatic narrative, provided here by the ever-changing influences on design, from technological innovations such as computers and tubular steel to the vagaries of royal taste and even, in the case of native walnut trees damaged by storms, the weather. He has a keen sense of the momentum of change, the dialectics of Gothick and Classical, of ornament and restraint, of finely detailed carpentry and rigorous Modernism. He plays these out against specific backdrops – Paxton's Crystal Palace, William Morris's Red House, the Bauhaus – using them as markers to remind us of the exhilaration of change.

Tim Gosling is authoritative, not just because he writes well, but because he makes fine furniture. What this book does is to present his argument that the design of everyday things, such as tables, chairs and the rooms we live in, should embody a sense of skill and integrity and beauty, and that this matters very much. I have already learned a lot from this persuasive, good-humoured and accessible book. I hope that many others will, too. For I agree with Tim: these things are important. After all, we are talking about making the world a better place.

Michael Palin

Introduction

I grew up being fascinated about how things worked and what made something … something. How do you capture the essence of design? What are the tell-tale clues that allow you to understand when it was made and to what stylistic period it belongs? Every chair we sit on can tell us a story through its structure and appearance, like folklore handed down through the ages: each piece can tell us when it was created and what the designer was trying to achieve. It is wonderful to realize that we are surrounded by these messages, encoded, as it were, within the DNA of furniture that we use every day.

My father, Raymond Gosling, took the first photograph of the double helix alongside Rosalind Franklin in 1950. They were both working on X-ray diffraction forms of highly hydrated DNA. It is perhaps not surprising, therefore, that I have often tried to identify the inherent visual aspects of furniture design – its 'DNA', if you will. If we can understand the basics of historic design as applied to furniture, we will be in a better position to break the rules, allowing us to continue moving design forward.

Within the chapters that follow, I have set out my personal thoughts on key design periods and on how my own work relates to them, highlighting some iconic interiors and pieces of furniture that, for me, capture the very essence of the time in which they were designed.

The Eighteenth Century

THE DESIGN RULES

· A taste for simplicity in decoration and design, which creates formality and grandeur ·
· Inspiration from Classical Greek and Roman architecture; the use of correct mouldings and the 'Greek key' and 'Vitruvian scroll' ·
· Distinctive carved motifs in furniture: the shell, the 'ball-and-claw' foot ·
· Fluidity of carved and gilded ornament ·
· The influence of chinoiserie in carving and lacquerwork ·
· Gothick motifs whimsically adapted from original architectural and decorative features of the Middle Ages ·

KEY PERIODS

Styles	Kings and Queens	Materials
Baroque (1660s–1720s)	Queen Anne (1702–1714)	Age of Walnut (1690s–1730s)
Palladian (1720s–1740s)	George I (1714–1727)	
Rococo / Chinoiserie /	George II (1727–1760)	
Gothick (1740s–1760s)		Age of Mahogany (1740s–1780s)
Neoclassical (1760s–1820s)	George III (1760–1820)	Age of Satinwood (1780s–1800s)

LEADING FIGURES

Sir Christopher Wren
[1632–1723]
Amateur architect of genius. He intended his monumental St Paul's Cathedral to be the centrepiece of a grandiose urban plan to rebuild London following the Great Fire in 1666.

Nicholas Hawksmoor
[1661–1736]
Wren's brilliant assistant, who later collaborated with Vanbrugh. Designer of churches in a Baroque classical manner, he added the iconic towers to the west front of Westminster Abbey.

Sir John Vanbrugh
[1664–1726]
Celebrated as both playwright and architect. Master of Baroque theatricality; his great houses include Castle Howard, Seaton Delaval and Blenheim Palace.

William Kent
[1685–1748]
Architect, furniture designer and landscape gardener. Works include Kensington Palace and Horse Guards Parade. The leading designer of interiors for great Palladian houses, such as Houghton and Holkham.

Richard Boyle, 3rd Earl of Burlington
[1694–1753]
Amateur architect, taste-maker and proponent of the Palladian style. His 'country villa' at Chiswick set a pattern for Augustan splendour.

Thomas Chippendale
[1718–1779]
Designer and furniture-maker working in the Rococo, Chinoiserie and Neoclassical styles; creator of the best-known of the pattern books, *The Gentleman and Cabinet-Maker's Director*.

Sir William Chambers
[1723–1796]
Versatile architect and favourite of George III; his range extended from the vast Neoclassical Somerset House to the fanciful Chinese pavilion in the gardens of Kew Palace.

George Hepplewhite
[1727–1786]
Furniture designer. Though no pieces can be attributed to his own workshop, the designs in his pattern book for stylish but relaxed and practical furnishings were widely followed.

Robert Adam
[1728–1792]
Master of simplified classical forms adorned with exquisitely moulded and coloured plasterwork, derived from his unrivalled knowledge of Roman architecture and decoration. Designed country houses and town palaces, but his great urban development, the Adelphi, was largely demolished.

Thomas Sheraton
[1751–1806]
Furniture designer; his influential pattern book was the first to include instructions on how to cost the manufacture of furnishings.

[page 10]
The main hallway of a contemporary
house in Sarasota, Florida, has a
hand-cut marquetry panel as its focal
point. It was created to extend the
perspective by continuing the line of
chandeliers on the architectural axis.
Its design is based on a palazzo
in Rome.

Old books on the history of English furniture are often rather like the furniture they describe: polished but now a bit creaky, perhaps a little outmoded but basically sound and still useful. As a designer, I love these volumes, which illustrate the finest – and sometimes the humblest – pieces from the past and show the appearance of long-vanished rooms; they have a certain magic about them and can offer the most wonderful inspiration. Unlike recent studies of English furniture and decoration, which tend to approach their subject largely in terms of stylistic development, older books tell a story that is more likely to be structured around the reigns of kings and queens. Even today, many auctioneers still use these convenient and well-understood regnal periods in their catalogue descriptions, referring to a Charles II chair, a Queen Anne looking-glass or a George III Pembroke table. This way of dating pieces certainly has its merits, since it can reveal the often overlooked significance of social and political factors in the history of design. In the early years of the eighteenth century, for example, the way the preferences in architecture and furnishings of Queen Anne's old Tory supporters were supplanted by the bold Palladian ideals of the new Whig aristocracy and the tastes of a rising, pro-Hanoverian merchant class marked a profound cultural shift.

An alternative but equally insightful way of structuring the story of English furniture was pioneered by the Edwardian artist, historian and antique collector Percy McQuoid, who based his chronological approach simply upon the type of wood predominantly used by furniture-makers in each era. McQuoid began his monumental sequence of works with *The Age of Oak,* published in 1904, and three further volumes followed swiftly: *The Age of Walnut* in 1905, *Mahogany* in 1907 and, last in the quartet, *Satinwood* in 1908. McQuoid's narrative moves in a stately progression – and with many digressions – across the centuries, proposing what remains, now more than a century on, a convenient, useful framework for understanding the sequence of English furniture.

According to McQuoid's divisions, from its beginnings in medieval times the Age of Oak lasted throughout the sixteenth century and for most of the seventeenth. During this extended period, the old Gothic shapes and decorative details, based on carpenters' ways of working, that had shaped the earliest English furniture gave way to the influence of Renaissance ideas. Makers gradually adopted classical forms and ornament, marrying these new and sometimes only half-understood elements to the older furniture types enshrined by a robust, insular tradition.

With a quickening of the pace of innovation in furniture types, construction methods and ornamentation, the eighteenth century presided over more rapid changes in styles and fashions than had ever been seen before. The Age of Walnut, which exploited to the full the decorative possibilities of veneers of that distinctively figured, honey-coloured wood, coincided with the reigns of Queen Anne and the first two Georges. But following the failure of sufficient supplies of matured timber (brought about by a blight that largely destroyed the indigenous tree stock), the use of walnut gave way to the Age of Mahogany. Plentiful supplies of fine-quality timber arriving from the New World ensured a widespread enthusiasm for mahogany that arose in the middle years of the century and continued in the ascendant through much of the reign of George III.

Mahogany, with its unfigured, small, even grain and rich brown tones, seemed to fit exactly the undemonstrative tastes of 'Farmer' George's court, and the practical and soberly furnished houses of English country gentlemen. But as the king's health and sanity failed, so this homely influence waned, and the new and flashier tastes in furnishings espoused by the Prince of Wales and his coterie came to the fore in more self-consciously fashionable circles. As a result, in the last decades of the eighteenth century the vogue for exquisitely refined and rarefied decoration, and a liking for lighter, brighter and more colourful decorative effects, led to the novel use of the pale, silky veneers – often with painted embellishments – that characterized the brief Age of Satinwood.

For McQuoid and other connoisseurs of his day, who abhorred any developments in taste after around 1800, the story of English furniture design more or less came to an end at this point. Though it is an obvious simplification of a highly complex chronology, as a practical maker I find McQuoid's concentration on the differing materials favoured over the years by craftsmen and their patrons very telling; for this reason, especially, his scheme of things as expressed in his four great books remains, for me, both appealing and instructive as a guide to the occasionally mysterious evolutions of taste and fashion.

Historians of architecture and connoisseurs and collectors of furniture have long agreed that the eighteenth century in England marked a high point in both design and craftsmanship. The Georgian era has been categorized as a period of supreme civilization, during which the restrained, classically inspired architecture and interiors of the English country house reached their finest expression. Similarly, the practical elegance of the tall terraced houses erected in such large numbers in towns and cities across the country was complemented by the beauty and utility of an unprecedented range of domestic goods. With its

sense of ordered calm, life in the eighteenth century – at least for those with the means to live well – had perhaps never been so agreeable.

This was an era in which the notion of 'taste' and the ideal of the 'man of taste' became of surpassing importance. Good taste – which by general consensus was understood to mean taste founded upon study of the classics, knowledge of history and an accomplished ability to judge pictures, ancient sculpture, landscapes and, of course, buildings – was held to be the essential attainment of the man of position and property. To foster these civilized virtues and to prepare them for the life they would be expected to lead, aristocratic and other privileged young men were sent on the Grand Tour: a journey combining education, sightseeing and social polishing that might last a year or two, or even longer. They followed a well-established route that included as its key stopping points the great centres of European civilization, including Paris, Venice, Florence and, as its culmination, Rome.

Usually accompanied by tutors, these 'travelling boys' were, whatever their social status, dubbed *milordi* by the Italians, who discovered a great many ways to exploit both their excitement at being abroad and their enthusiasm for buying art. Bringing home with them souvenirs and, frequently, genuine artistic treasures – Greek vases and other archaeological objects, rare books and, in particular, Roman statuary and Old Master paintings (though the last two often proved to be copies recently manufactured in Italy) – the young travellers returned ready to inherit grand country houses and 'town palaces'. Their tastes had been honed, enabling them to fill their properties with well-chosen collections and to furnish them in the latest fashion. The English country house, that most revered creation of the era, and the 'country house style', which remains even

Giovanni Paolo Pannini, *Picture Gallery with Views of Modern Rome*, 1757. The young men who undertook the Grand Tour were enthusiastic collectors – much to the Italians' delight.

[opposite]
Robert Dennis Chantrell, *Perspective
of the Staircase at 44 Berkeley Square,
London*, 1813. Designed by William Kent
in the 1740s, this staircase was used
as the inspiration for the entrance hall
on page 24.

[left]
The Marble Hall at Holkham Hall,
Norfolk, showing the Vitruvian scroll
and contrasting marbles of the colonnade.

today a potent and enduring influence on design and decoration, both bear the unmistakable stamp of the Grand Tour.

From the time of Inigo Jones, who had spent perhaps six years studying the new architecture in Italy around 1600, to that of Christopher Wren, whose enlightenment came during a shorter but no less fruitful sojourn in France, foreign travel played the most important part in the education of would-be architects. In the seventeenth century most architects were still gentlemen amateurs; the greatest among them, such as Wren or the playwright and courtier Sir John Vanbrugh, could be said to have relied as much on individual genius and imagination as on any real systematic study. In addition, much of the domestic building of the period, some of it of extremely high quality and showing a surprising degree of architectural sophistication, had been left to local practitioners or to the traditional, inherited skills of the master-mason. By the beginning of the eighteenth century we certainly begin to see a new degree of professionalism coming in, but it is only by the middle years of the century that it is possible to talk of a proper architectural profession.

Among the many brilliant architects at work during this period, several also excelled as designers of furniture and schemes of interior decoration. The work of two men in particular, William Kent and Robert Adam, has always been especially inspirational for me, for both the range of the projects they undertook and their extraordinary attention to detail. Each, in their different ways, reveals the importance of always considering the total effect. For Kent and Adam, all the elements – from the architectural space itself to the precise form of mouldings and ornament, and not only the design, but also the placing of every piece of furniture – contribute to, are indeed essential to, the success of the whole.

Kent, who trained initially as a painter, created some of the finest interiors of the first half of the century. His major works included schemes for the royal palaces of Kensington and Hampton Court, while his interiors for several of the most important new country houses, including Houghton for Sir Robert Walpole and Holkham for Thomas Coke, Earl of Leicester, represent the most important statements of the Palladian ideal. In all these interiors Kent's massive, grandiose but architecturally correct furniture, with its carved and gilded ornament, was played off against richly coloured wall treatments to create an allusion to Roman grandeur within an ambience of thoroughly modern, opulent luxury.

The architectural projects, interiors and furnishings by Adam also play upon Roman themes and prototypes but are altogether cooler, more self-consciously Neoclassical. Adam spent a lengthy time in Italy, thereby earning for himself the nickname 'Bob the Roman'. During this period he thoroughly imbibed the spirit of ancient Roman architecture and also, as far as it was possible, studied examples of carved and moulded stucco work that had survived. He stored a vast repertoire of forms and patterns in extensive volumes of drawings (now preserved in Sir John Soane's Museum, London) that served as models for the exquisitely modulated decoration of town houses and country house interiors upon which his reputation rests.

Although Neoclassical ideals in their various guises were close to all-pervasive in the most fashionable circles, it is by no means the case that any single style or set of design values obtained throughout the century. Indeed, one of the great charms of the period is its pleasing multiplicity of stylistic possibilities – a diversity that ranges from the robust, Roman-inspired architecture and massive furniture of the early years to the chaste and delicate classicism of the later decades.

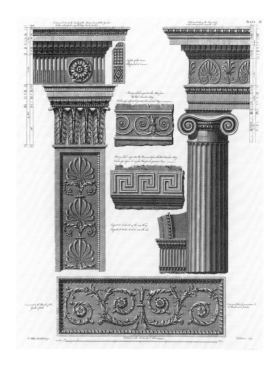

It embraces with equal enthusiasm the delicate and inventive frivolities of the Gothick and chinoiserie tastes so redolent of the 1740s to the 1760s.

Both chinoiserie and the Gothick were viewed as somewhat anti-establishment styles, their fantasy and playfulness being irrational, outside the rules and often characterized as 'feminine'. Chinoiserie had the older history, having first been popular in the seventeenth century, when blue and white china, stamped leathers and 'japanning', which copied oriental lacquer decoration, were the essential ingredients. Eighteenth-century chinoiserie, by contrast, was lighter in effect; it made great use of expensive imported painted Chinese wallpapers – or their cheaper English-made imitations – and matched their prettiness with deliberately fragile-looking furniture, often painted, gilded and ornamented with fretwork. Among the leading exponents of this kind of ultra-fashionable fantasy furnishing was Thomas Chippendale, who offered not only elaborate, gilded looking-glasses and girandoles ornamented with pagodas and 'ho-ho birds', but also much simpler painted pieces, such as an entire suite of bedroom furniture supplied to the celebrated actor David Garrick for his riverside villa.

Eighteenth-century Gothick (usually spelled with a 'k' to distinguish it from the true medieval style) was also seen at first as not merely fanciful but subversive. Among the leading proponents of the movement was Horace Walpole, who in the 1740s created his own riverside villa near Garrick's at Twickenham. It has been said that Walpole sought to 're-create the Middle Ages in miniature'; indeed, he famously described Strawberry Hill as his 'little plaything castle'. Part pleasure-house and part setting for his extraordinary collection of pictures, china, antiquities and historical portraits and curiosities, the house was open to the public, thereby making its name synonymous with the new Gothick taste. Although he furnished it with some ancient and exotic pieces, such as Indo-Portuguese carved ebony chairs from Goa, of the type that connoisseurs of the day mistook for English Tudor, Walpole also commissioned new pieces in an appropriate style. His famous set of black dining chairs, their backs modelled on Gothic window tracery, was designed by the most inventive member of Walpole's 'Committee of Taste', the artist Richard Bentley. They were supplied by Hallett, one of the leading London furniture-makers of the day. If these were uncompromising, elsewhere Walpole introduced 'plump sofas'; 'In truth,' he wrote, 'I did not mean to make my house so Gothic as to exclude convenience, and modern refinements in luxury. The designs of the inside and outside are strictly ancient, but the decoration is modern.'

For me, one of the greatest revelations in visiting Strawberry Hill today is Walpole's exceptional use of light and shade, the controlled 'gloom' of the medieval alongside the stained-glass colours that still saturate the floors and walls at different times of day with the most dazzling blues, reds, greens and pinks.

Meeting the challenge of creating furnishings with style and grace, and devising interiors in which the new 'luxury goods' could be displayed and enjoyed to the full, the period saw the rise of a new kind of designer whose skills perfectly complemented those of the architects of the day. The genius of men such as Chippendale, Sheraton and Hepplewhite – that great trio of English eighteenth-century makers – was not only expressed in the products made by their own fashionable workshops, but also spread through the relatively novel means of illustrated 'pattern books', or collections of designs. These

[opposite, left]
The Kimbolton Cabinet, designed by Robert Adam in 1771–76, contains exceptional pietra dura plaques by the Florentine Baccio Cappelli. The mounts are by Matthew Bolton, and the cabinetmaker was Ince of London.

[opposite, right]
Details of Robert Adam's designs for the south front at Kenwood House, London, from the *Works in Architecture of Robert and James Adam* (1774). They were used by Gosling for the frieze panel on the hall table on pages 22–23.

[below]
Thomas Sandby, Paul Sandby and Edward Edwards, *The Gallery at Strawberry Hill*, *c.* 1765–81. The house at Strawberry Hill, Twickenham, was created by Horace Walpole, one of the leading proponents of the Gothick movement.

volumes featuring designs for all manner of furnishings, printed in meticulous detail from engraved copperplates, were avidly studied by rich patrons and the smarter London furniture-makers alike, but they also carried the new fashions to a vast number of industrious craftsmen in the provincial centres of Britain and even abroad. These pattern books remain a valuable resource for designers who seek insights and inspiration from the past for their own work.

It is both fascinating and instructive to trace the wide-reaching influence of Thomas Chippendale in particular. Chippendale was one of the leading London tradesmen of his day, supplying furniture and decorative furnishings to clients all over the country. *The Gentleman and Cabinet-Maker's Director,* his handsomely produced collection of 160 engraved plates, which first appeared in 1754, became the most celebrated of all eighteenth-century pattern books. Although the *Director* offered a sparkling compendium of all that was fashionable and stylish, in his pieces Chippendale always reined in the most frivolous of Rococo or chinoiserie flourishes with a distinctly English robustness; perhaps, above all, it was this subtle combination of utility with appropriate and graceful ornamentation that made Chippendale's designs for both grand and more everyday pieces so popular.

Certainly Chippendale's ideas were extraordinarily widely followed, for while there are perhaps a mere six hundred or so pieces that can be securely documented as authentic productions of his St Martin's Lane workshop, many thousands of splat-back chairs, fretwork cabinets and other items of furniture that are based directly on his designs survive. And, in addition to these pieces that reproduce his designs with accuracy (and are generically called 'Chippendale'), many more humble, provincial-made pieces and cottage furnishings of the

middle and later years of the eighteenth century reveal his unmistakable influence – though often charmingly misunderstood and misapplied by country furniture-makers and estate carpenters.

Beyond the shores of the United Kingdom, Chippendale's ideas also gained currency. It is recorded, perhaps rather unexpectedly, that Catherine the Great had Chippendale's *Director* in her library in St Petersburg, and that Louis XVI of France possessed a copy of an edition published in French in 1762. More predictably, in Georgian Dublin and in the prosperous Eastern centres of colonial America, craftsmen whose skills matched and even surpassed those of the London makers gave their own particular ornamental flourishes to Chippendale's designs. Irish furniture of the mid-eighteenth century is justly celebrated for its spirited and imaginative carving.

While looking at examples of what is often described as 'American Chippendale', however, I am always intrigued to note that these variations are so idiosyncratic that experts can identify with some certainty whether pieces originate from Boston or New York, Newport or Philadelphia, or even from which workshop. Each one had its own distinctive manner of carving details such as the decorative shell motifs found on the apron of side-tables and the bases of high-boys, or of treating the claw on the ball-and-claw foot.

This tell-tale detail, the ball-and-claw foot, was a curious form that enjoyed great popularity with English cabinetmakers in the first half of the century. According to tradition, it derived from the Oriental symbolic motif (seen in embroideries, on painted vases and elsewhere) of the imperial dragon clutching in its claw the flaming pearl of wisdom and purity. By 1754 it was already too outmoded a feature to be included by Chippendale

[opposite]
Chinoiserie at Nostell Priory, Yorkshire, decorated by Thomas Chippendale in 1769. The Dressing Room has hand-painted wallpaper imported from China depicting birds, trees and flowers.

[below]
Example of an American Chippendale side chair with ball-and-claw feet, 1765–75. The ball-and-claw foot is derived from the Asian motif of an imperial dragon clutching in its claw a flaming pearl.

in his book, but it remained popular with the makers of 'American Chippendale' pieces well into the latter part of the century. It is fascinating to realize that, although the motif remains synonymous with his style and work, Chippendale never actually included it in his *Director*.

Today, looking through the pages of Chippendale's *Director*, I am constantly struck by the inventiveness of his designs, and especially by the way in which his ornamentation – whether rich and elaborate or, as it often is, more modest – emerges organically, seeming to grow naturally from the structural forms of his pieces. Whether carved crisply or further picked out by gilding, these ornamental flourishes enrich and emphasize the mouldings and, by contrast, reveal the beauty of the plain surfaces in a way that is curiously satisfying and pleasing both to the eye and to the hand. As designer of furniture and interiors – working in whichever style – I hope always to achieve something similar. Following my heroes and illustrious predecessors in the eighteenth century – William Kent, Robert Adam and others – I base my work and, indeed, my entire philosophy of design on the ideal that architecture is our great source of inspiration and the fount of all authority in our creative processes. So I was especially delighted to discover that, in the introductory remarks to the *Director,* Chippendale expressed an idea that neatly complements my own belief: 'Of all the arts which are either improved or ornamented by Architecture,' he wrote, 'that of CABINET-MAKING is not only the most useful and ornamental, but capable of receiving as great assistance from it as any whatever.' That 'assistance' is crucial: it is by knowing, understanding and, just occasionally, breaking the architectural rules that we are enabled to create individual pieces and the interior settings fit for them which possess that essential sense of order, proportion and beauty.

[left]
Detail of the staircase showing the 'S'-shaped scroll design of the ironwork, the mahogany handrail and the balustrade finial.

[opposite]
The entrance hall of the house in Sarasota, with its double-cube proportions and Italianate window and arch designs. This room was based on William Kent's drawings from his trips to Italy.

[opposite]
A desk made in santos rosewood, with inlays of brass designed to echo the architecture of the house. The exterior colonnade can be seen through the window.

[right]
The desk pavilions are made from santos rosewood and feature miniature carved and water-gilded Italianate capitals.

[following pages]
The dining room table and sideboards all feature elements based on Robert Adam's designs. They are framed by three spectacular double-barrel vaults.

[left]
Detail of the mahogany sideboard in Sarasota. Instead of making the uprights of brass or wood, as is traditional, Gosling chose to create them in fluted acrylic and glass. This preserves the strength of the Adam form, but results in a more contemporary piece, lighter in feel.

[below left]
The exceptional hand-carving of the scroll legs and deep-cut acanthus leaves add to the fluidity of the sideboard, which is hung on the wall to avoid the need for any additional supporting legs.

[opposite]
The frieze of the dining table is in water-gilded platinum (silver leaf would be at risk of oxidizing and darkening). It features hand-carved triglyph motifs. The supporting columns are a strong Doric design with deep fluting, and they rest on slightly raised quadripartite bases.

[below right]
The sideboard is designed very precisely so that its upper frame curves up to meet the mirror above. The curves of the sideboard's profile match those of the upper section and add to a feeling of lightness and balance.

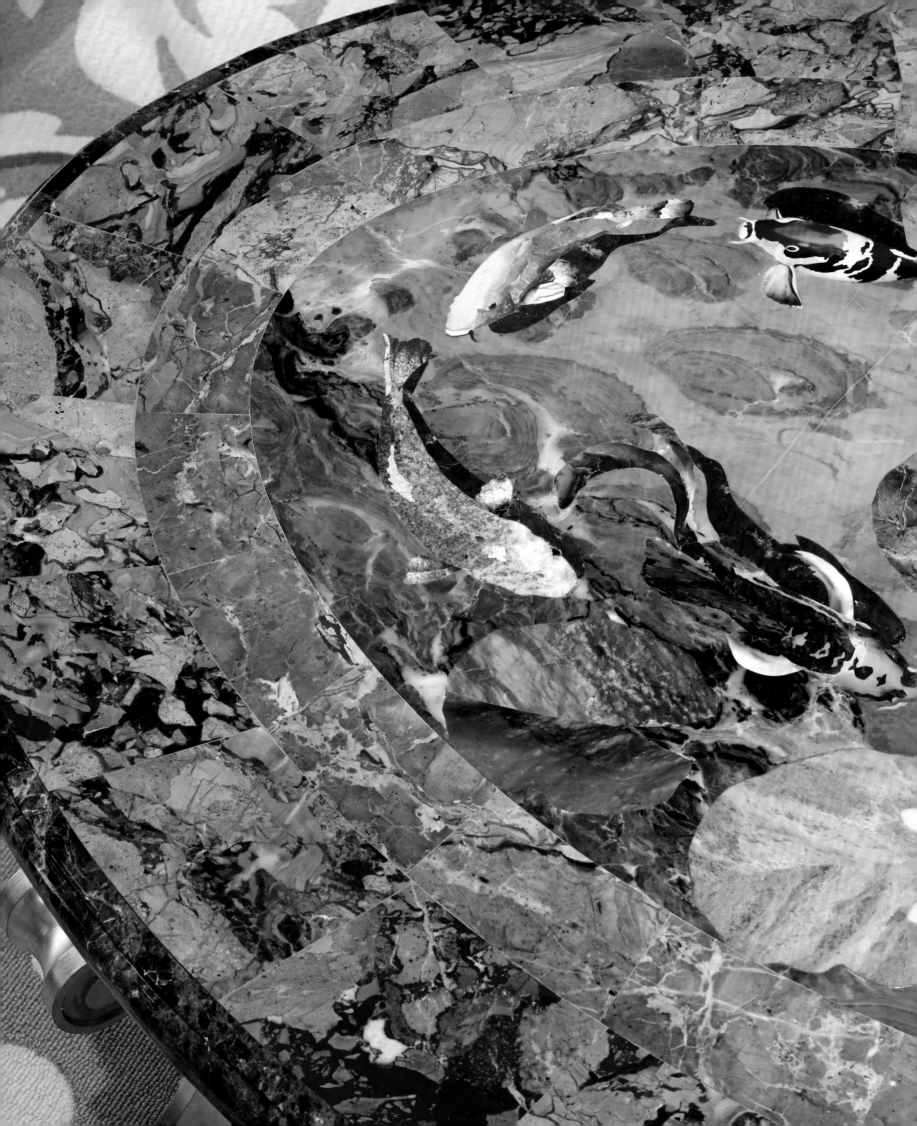

[opposite]
Detail of the low pietra dura table, made from hundreds of pieces of precious hand-cut marbles and stones, in the house in Sarasota. The extraordinary shading is created in much the same way as it is with wood, by burning the edges to create an exceptional three-dimensional effect. These koi carp appear to be swimming in water.

[right]
The pietra dura table top is supported by a hand-carved, water-gilded frame. Its frieze is made using cross-grained American walnut to work tonally with the marbles and to create a strong horizontal plane, thus integrating the top with its gilded base.

[preceding pages]
This exceptional pietra dura panel by Pitti Mosaici in the house in Sarasota is based on a large shutter panel in the Museo dell'Opificio delle Pietre Dure, Florence, made in 1879. The careful deployment of hundreds of pieces of hand-cut and shaded stones – including the sensational 'jaune de Sienne' yellow marble – succeeds in creating not only a floral bouquet, but also the illusion that a vase sits on the real water-gilded half-moon table. The panel was split into two sections so that the console table could be cantilevered off the wall.

[below]
This mahogany circular dining table in my dining room in London sits on a fluted column on a raised quadripartite base. The top is made from ebony inlaid into slip-matched flame mahogany. A series of eight Romanoff crests have been inlaid into the ebony using a traditional Boulle technique.

[opposite]
Close-up showing the double-headed Romanoff crests in polished brass inlaid into the ebony banding on the table top. Their design was based on a set of engraved glasses brought back from St Petersburg.

Regency
1800–1830

THE DESIGN RULES

· A strong sense of formal symmetry ·
· Use of classical forms, such as capitals, columns and fluted pedestals ·
· Carved decoration contrasting with plain surfaces ·
· Classical motifs derived from stylized plant forms, such as the palmette or anthemion ·
· Use of mahogany, flame-mahogany and rosewood, with inlays of richly figured and coloured woods
such as calamander and zebrana ·
· Decorative motifs drawn from ancient Greek and Roman architecture, but also from 'exotic' sources:
Egypt, India and China ·
· Gothick forms and details used to evoke the romantic feel of the past ·

MATERIALS

Mahogany
Santos rosewood, Rio rosewood, Bombay rosewood
Ormolu (mercury-gilded cast bronze)
Gilded and painted details
Solid Indian ebony
Veneers
Boulle inlays (fretted brass)

LEADING FIGURES

Henry Holland
[1745–1806]
Partner and son-in-law of Capability Brown.
Architect of the early phases of the Prince
Regent's Carlton House and Brighton Pavilion.
Famous London buildings include Brooks's Club
and the Albany. His finest country house,
Southill, exemplifies his refined classical manner.
John Soane was one of his apprentices.

James Wyatt
[1746–1813]
Architect of the splendid Pantheon, Oxford
Street, in the classical style, and of Fonthill
Abbey. This grandest of Gothick houses was so
hastily built that it collapsed in 1825.

Thomas Sheraton
[1751–1806]
Furniture designer. His pattern books included
the four-volume *Cabinet-Maker's and
Upholsterer's Drawing-Book* (1791); it was
subscribed to by 600 cabinetmakers and became
the leading style manual of the day. Later books
contained measurements and working drawings
to elucidate furniture-making techniques.

John Nash
[1752–1835]
The Prince Regent's favourite architect, for
whom he worked on Carlton House, Brighton
Pavilion and Buckingham Palace. A prolific
builder, he devised the prince's grandiose urban
development stretching between Regent's Park
and Regent Street, and also produced picturesque
castle-style country houses.

Sir John Soane
[1753–1837]
Highly inventive, experimental architect. His
Dulwich Picture Gallery established a pattern for
public art collections. His best-loved work is his
own house in Lincoln's Inn Fields (now a
museum), in which his astonishing collections are
displayed in small interlinked rooms. Signature
detailing includes the use of flat ebony strips in
place of raised mouldings, and reflective strips of
mirror-glass to multiply vistas. He never received
royal commissions, but at the zenith of his career
designed the Bank of England complex (now
sadly spoiled by later insensitive alteration).

Nicholas Morel
[1759–1830]
Furniture-maker and upholsterer who executed
Henry Holland's designs for Carlton House and
Brighton Pavilion. He joined George Seddon
(1796–1857) to form the leading firm of the day.

Thomas Hope
[1769–1831]
Banker, author, collector and amateur architect.
He designed furniture in ancient Greek and
Egyptian styles, but angered fashionable London
when he issued tickets to view his mansion.

George Bullock
[1782–1818]
Furniture-maker whose sumptuous pieces are
characterized by their use of intricately fretted
brass inlays and other rich materials.

Decimus Burton
[1800–1881]
Architect of the Wellington Arch and the
Athenaeum Club, London, which he designed at
the age of 24. He was the protégé of John Nash
and the tenth son of James Burton (1761–1837).

'There is something daring about Regency furniture, something which makes one's friends exclaim "how exciting".' Writing in the 1930s, Christopher Hussey, the editor of *Country Life* magazine and something of an architectural taste-maker, caught the mood of his day precisely. Jaded with the insipid minimalism of the Modern Movement, a new generation of clever young architects, interior designers and collectors were rediscovering the fascination of the Regency period. They revelled in its inventive and often wildly experimental forms, in its unabashed use of the richest of materials, and its love of bright, saturated colour. I am constantly amazed at, and delighted by, these aspects of Regency design, and find inspiration for my own work in the period's verve and daring.

The Regency period is still in many ways defined by the style and artistic mood set by George, Prince of Wales, and is customarily taken to embrace not only the years of his father's madness, during which he served as Regent, but also the decade of his own reign as George IV from 1820 to 1830. Where George III had been quiet, uxorious, homely or even frugal, the Prince – known ubiquitously as 'Prinny' – was hedonistic and fond of luxury and fast company. As a collector and patron of the arts, he was passionate about pictures, gilded furniture, ormolu and the finest porcelain. He was also recklessly enthusiastic in his plans for new building works and schemes of decoration for the royal palaces; these extravagances left him almost constantly in debt and at odds with his ministers over the royal finances.

In my opinion, George engendered some of the most wonderful palaces, interiors and furniture designs of all time. And while his works at Windsor Castle and Buckingham Palace, both of which he remodelled extensively and at very great expense, might ultimately be judged more grandiose than imaginatively inspired, in the case of Carlton House and the Pavilion at Brighton the Prince gave free rein to his most brilliant architects and designers, including Henry Holland, James Wyatt and John Nash, and thereby achieved two undoubted architectural and decorative masterpieces.

Carlton House was given to the Prince on his twenty-first birthday in 1783 as his official London residence and remained so for some forty years. No longer in existence, it is one of the most intriguing 'lost' palaces of England; but perhaps for this very reason it still tantalizes by the way it hints at fascinating episodes in the development of taste in an era of conspicuous style and extravagance. In fact, the house was begun in a chaste, French-inspired style by Henry Holland. Later it underwent many changes as George's enthusiasm for gilded grandeur and exoticism developed. At different points its complex history, Greek and Roman classical details coexisted with Gothick, while one drawing room – known from illustrations in Thomas Sheraton's celebrated pattern book – revealed the beginnings of the Prince's influential espousal of the chinoiserie style.

Ultimately, in spite of the fortune he had spent on the near continual remodelling of the architectural spaces, renewal of the decoration and additions to the furnishings, George demolished what had become an inconvenient home, selling off both the site and such building materials as could be salvaged. It has been suggested that the constricted site on which the palace and its gardens stood offered insufficient possibilities for his ever grander schemes, but also that endless, uncoordinated alterations had rendered the building actually unsafe. Another, quite plausible reason was that George – never a popular figure – had grown nervous of living, as it was said, just 'a stone's throw' from the public thoroughfare. However, financial

[opposite]
A Regency-period watercolour from Pierce Egan's *Life in London* (1823). Aside from many wonderful watercolours of rooms and furniture, the book features the escapades of Corinthian Tom, interestingly illustrated here in a 'Corinthian Capital'.

[below]
The glamorous Rose Satin Drawing Room of Carlton House, London, as engraved by Richard Reeve in William Henry Pyne's *The History of the Royal Residences* (1816–19).

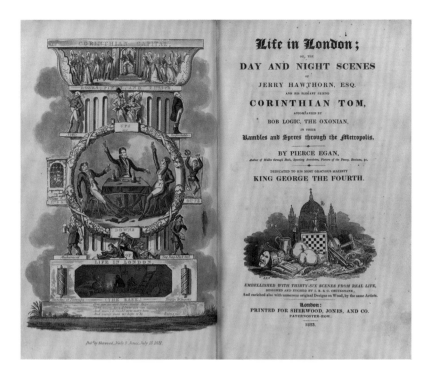

exigencies undoubtedly also played the key part in his decision to abandon the house, for even after his accession George was still mired in considerable debts and now also faced the necessity of rebuilding the ramshackle apartments of old Buckingham House as a properly functioning royal palace. Fortunately, we know a great deal about Carlton House's appearance from the magnificent coloured aquatint plates based on detailed watercolours by Charles Wild in the sumptuous volumes of William Henry Pyne's *The History of the Royal Residences*, published in 1816–19. In these glamorous images it is possible to recognize many individual pieces of furniture and other objects that subsequently moved from their original positions at Carlton House to Brighton and thence to Buckingham Palace, where many remain to this day.

Similarly inspiring are the coloured prints – of which I am lucky enough to own a full set – documenting the appearance of the Regent's 'Marine Pavilion at Brighthelmstone', or Brighton Pavilion as we now know it. Here a similar trajectory can be traced in the various stages of building and decoration, from initial classical sobriety to over-the-top exoticism masterminded by the royal favourite, John Nash. As the crowning glory of Nash's vision, the Pavilion in fact brought together a number of heterogeneous architectural styles, imaginatively and fearlessly mixed. For the exterior massing and ornamentation, Nash enriched the plain façades of the relatively modest original core of the building with a brilliant confection of 'Hindoo', Mughal and other Indian elements, as well as Turkish details. As Nash's contemporary and rival Thomas Hopper aptly put it: 'It is the architect's job to be master of all styles and partial in favour of none.'

Internally, the rooms of the Pavilion vary, according to scale and intended use, from a gentle, rather eighteenth-century style of chinoiserie, based around imported Chinese painted wallpapers, soft silks and delicate lacquered and painted furniture, through to the bombastic, almost overwhelming theatricality of the great set-piece apartments such as the dining and music rooms. In these – the highest and largest spaces, at either end of the structure – the effects are quite extraordinary, with riotous colour and lavish carving and gilding pointed up by spectacular lighting from then highly novel gas chandeliers made of mirror-glass and crystal. In its heyday as the seaside retreat of the 'Prince of Pleasure', the Pavilion was filled with a tremendous array of objects; these ranged from the gloriously fantastical, such as life-size 'nodding mandarins' and ceramic pagodas 3 metres (10 feet) high, to practical furniture, silver, porcelain and glass tableware of the very highest workmanship. Today, I find its extraordinary inventiveness, its wit and its staggering quality of execution both awesome and inspiring.

When compared with the cultured but very deliberately modest life chosen by his parents, George III and Queen Charlotte, the Prince Regent's opulent taste and extravagant spending led to him being seen as the ultimate leader of fashion. He was, however, by no means the only extravagant builder or obsessive collector of his era. Many aristocrats of the day lavished their wealth on refurbishing old family homes and estates or building new houses on a grand scale. Outside the ranks of the nobility, men such as William Beckford and the banker Thomas Hope offered a clear challenge to the Regent's position as *arbiter elegantiarum*.

Beckford, heir to a sugar-plantation fortune that made him, for a while at least, 'England's wealthiest son', built the astounding Fonthill Abbey, a Gothick folly designed by James Wyatt on an unimaginably vast scale. Its galleries, which were 91 metres (300 feet) long, were intersected by a tower topped

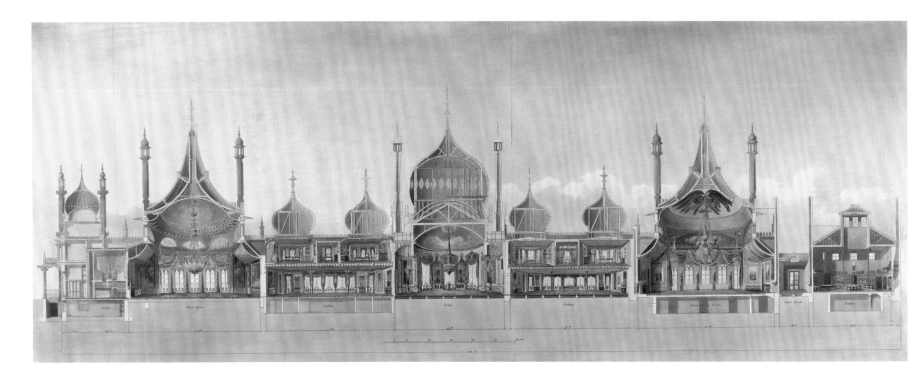

with a spire the size of that at Salisbury Cathedral. Indefatigable in his search of books, pictures, rare cabinets and priceless pieces of furniture, Beckford not only bought at all the celebrated auction sales of his day, but even travelled incognito to Paris during the most dangerous time of the Terror in order to secure treasures displaced from the royal palaces of France.

Thomas Hope, equally enamoured of French stylishness and quality, numbered among his friends the greatest of contemporary French architects and furniture designers, Charles Percier and Pierre-François-Léonard Fontaine. In the furnishings he himself designed for his London mansion in Duchess Street, Hope introduced his own version of their distinctive, archaeologically inspired Neoclassicism. This style, which dominated French taste during the Directoire period of the Revolution and in the days of Napoleon's Empire, can be characterized as masculine and opulent. It also relied in particular on the use of classical motifs, including lion's-paw feet, masks, paterae (dish-like roundels) and stars, and details such as frets and scrolls drawn from the repertoire of Egyptian and ancient Greek architecture. Intriguingly, though they were seldom employed on the grandiose scale that Hope considered appropriate to his town palace, such design ideas – once refined in elegance and reduced to a more manageable, domestic scale – would form the basis of much of the best 'ordinary' furniture of the Regency period. Hope's furniture was once described disparagingly as 'such a mass of squared timber as would sink the floor of a London house'; by contrast, the standard Regency dining chair, with its slim sabre legs and perhaps a back of 'klismos' form inspired by the same Grecian aesthetic, is a thing of delicate beauty but surprising strength.

During this time the furnishing of ordinary houses of middling size and standing often reached a good level of workmanship and a surprising degree of visual sophistication when compared with that of other eras. This seems to me the more remarkable when it is borne in mind that, throughout the period from 1793 through to 1815, Britain was continually at war with France, with only the briefest respite during the year of the fragile Peace of Amiens in 1802–3; even after the Battle of Waterloo the country at first remained slumped in economic depression. In rural areas and in the towns and cities, the complex consequences of the Industrial Revolution led to widespread stirrings of unrest. Calls for social and political reform became more strident as consciousness grew of the great disparity in wealth between the landed aristocracy and the increasingly successful and assertive trade-oriented middle-classes on the one hand, and the old agrarian poor and the new shifting, urban, factory-working population on the other. Against this uneasy backdrop of a changing world order, serious discontent erupted from time to time in various areas, the worst incident being the infamous Peterloo Massacre of 1819: a 60,000-strong demonstration in Manchester that ended with the troops sent in by the authorities injuring 700 and causing the deaths of eleven protesters. However, in spite of this volatile atmosphere, the Regency period saw quite a boom in building, especially in towns where terraces of distinctively elegant houses sprang up in large numbers, and in the creation of a new, far broader-based market for furnishings and other luxury goods.

This was an era in which traditional crafts and the beginnings of mass production existed side-by-side, and both were informed, as never before, by a burgeoning market in pattern books and a growing range of illustrated publications intended to guide taste. One of the most enterprising print and book publishers of the day, Rudolph Ackermann, presided over a profitable and highly influential emporium, 'The Repository

[opposite]
John Nash's Royal Pavilion at Brighton (1815–22), here depicted in hand-coloured aquatint plate bound into an elephant folio for the Prince Regent's guests at the Pavilion.

[below]
Nash's exotic Banqueting Room for the Royal Pavilion. Many of the original wall panels are now reconfigured in the Chinese Dining Room at Buckingham Palace. This print served as a colour palette for the chinoiserie-style embroidery illustrated on pages 228–29.

[below and opposite]
Three plates from George Smith's *Cabinet Maker's and Upholsterer's Guide* (1826), one of the most influential books on decoration to be printed during the Regency period. They include a chart (opposite, left) showing the new colours of chrome yellow, arsenic green and puce (named after the colour of a squashed flea).

PLATE CL.

INTERIOR DECORATION.

Roman.

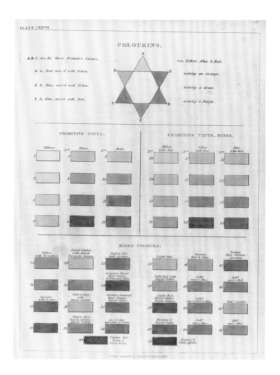

of Arts' in Regent Street, London. Between 1809 and 1829 he issued a monthly journal with coloured illustrations that played a crucial role in the dissemination of new ideas and evolving fashions in dress, interior decoration and furniture design. Within its pages, in a sequence of exquisite images redolent of the world of Jane Austen's heroines, those anxious to keep abreast of the latest trends could find inspiration for every aspect of polite existence, ranging from the newest day dresses of sprigged muslin and Indian shawls to elaborate curtain treatments and the first tentative designs for spiky Gothick furniture by the young Augustus Pugin.

So great was the demand for novel ideas for furnishings and authoritative guidance in matters of taste for those planning their own decorative schemes that almost every year of the Regency period saw new books of designs issued by tradesmen, professional designers, furniture-makers and even 'gentlemen amateurs' such as Thomas Hope. Hope's magnificent volume, which appeared in 1807, was based entirely on the grand Neoclassical designs of his Duchess Street mansion. Its title, *Household Furniture and Interior Decoration*, brought the latter term into use. Even more influential was the furniture designer George Smith's *Cabinet Maker's and Upholsterer's Guide*, published towards the end of the period, in 1826. Smith's 150 plates offered suggestions for sumptuous rooms adorned with lavish soft furnishings trimmed with elaborate and costly *passementerie*, and for useful and beautiful furniture for every part of a dwelling. Also included were patterns for highly ingenious items of 'metamorphic' furniture, such as a chair that transformed into library steps. I love the subtle cleverness of such pieces, from which we can still learn today.

Significantly, too, Smith gave authoritative instructions for the mixing and use of colour in decoration. As I suggested

earlier, for me Regency colour is always exhilarating. While the eighteenth-century palette included a few strong, though not always stable, colours, technical advances in paint manufacture offered Regency decorators and designers new possibilities. Recently invented chemical colours such as chrome yellow (first discovered in 1797) and the infamous arsenic greens (one of which may have led to Napoleon being poisoned by his wallpaper on the island of St Helena) allowed the creation of striking effects.

Fashion was influenced not only by these scientific advances in paints and dyes, but also by the rediscovery of the painted decoration of the ancient world. The archaeological exploration of Pompeii revealed complete schemes of Roman wall painting for the first time and created a sensation. The two handsome volumes of Sir William Gell's *Pompeiana* appeared in 1817–18 and inspired many designers, including Thomas Hope and the learned architect Sir John Soane, whose own London drawing room, painted in a brilliant Pompeian red with contrasting ornamental elements in bronze-green, still survives as a testament to the Regency era's love affair with the exotic past.

Since I take particular interest in the work of furniture designers and cabinetmakers of the past, I have always been fascinated by the evolution of fashions in the use of different woods. In the eighteenth century cabinetmakers had discovered the huge potential of Caribbean mahogany as a substitute when the supply of native walnut faltered after the great destruction of large trees by storms in 1730. Mahogany and another beautifully figured reddish wood, rosewood (itself now increasingly hard to source), became the favoured materials for much Regency furniture at all levels of society. For a London town house I created a stylish, distinctly Regency feel by using

both Bombay and santos rosewoods; the two timbers look spectacular together.

It is interesting to note the ways in which the Regency period's love of exotic styles, such as Egyptian, Greek or Gothick, and its use of vibrant colour are both mirrored directly in a contemporaneous taste for rare and fantastically figured woods. During the first decades of the nineteenth century we find such woods as zebrana, calamander, flame mahogany and the many differing species of ebony all employed to tremendous decorative effect. Normally used as veneers rather than in the solid (a technique brought to perfection around this time), these materials work well when contrasted with the warm red of mahogany or with paler woods. Similarly, the inlaying of lines (stringing) and other decorative motifs in brass, ivory, bone, pale holly or other woods stained green added a richness and elegance to many pieces. The French taste for cast and chased ornaments in dull brass or mercury-gilded bronze (ormolu) was taken up in England, especially for such pieces as cabinets and chairs in the classical style. Even the use of faux finishes, including painted simulations of the distinctive grain of rosewood, became fashionable, and some simple pieces, such as cane-seated chairs in more common woods, were painted black or picked out in delicious colours.

Another aspect of the period that intrigues me is the extent to which changes in taste and fashion became very much more rapid than in previous eras. This was true at all levels of the design world, from the very top end down to country-made chairs and tables. When choosing the furnishings and decoration for Apsley House – the gift of a grateful nation to the victor of Waterloo – the Duke of Wellington largely followed the established fashion in London town houses for a

relatively restrained Neoclassical taste, but also, perhaps surprisingly, spiced up some of his rooms with mouldings and other elements in a rather more avant-garde or, one might even say, flashy Rococo revival manner. His justification for the decision is significant: this was, he claimed (somewhat snobbishly), a style of decoration that unequivocally declared a man's status, since unlike almost all others it could never be imitated cheaply.

In my own work, I like to think that I draw inspiration from both the grandest creations of the great Regency architects and designers, emulating their use of the richest materials, and from the simpler, more everyday pieces of the period, whose charm lies in formal symmetry, restrained use of pattern and ornament and, above all, elegance of line. In its range of effects, from simplicity to grandeur, and in its constant search for beauty and refinement, Regency never disappoints.

[opposite, above]
The south end of the library at Sir John Soane's Museum, London, painted in the distinctive Pompeian red.

[opposite, below]
Pair of tables made for Thomas Hope's house in Duchess Street, London, after one of his designs published in the early nineteenth century. The lion monopodia were based on Roman designs that Hope knew and that in turn inspired my own versions (see page 60).

[right]
Plate from William Gell's *Pompeiana* (1817–19), created when the city of Pompeii was newly excavated. Sadly, many of the wall paintings' original colours have now faded or disappeared completely, owing to their exposure to the elements.

[preceding pages]
This circular Regency-style hall table for a Georgian town house in Belgravia was made in raw mahogany with edging of solid ebony. Santos rosewood was slip-matched to create a repeated, balanced pattern. All the points meet perfectly in the centre, which from a technical point of view is difficult to achieve.

[below]
The table opens to reveal several sealed humidor drawers made in traditional unfinished oak, so that the sides can be waxed for perfectly smooth running. The edge of the table is made from a thick band of solid ebony. The table was designed together with Joanna Wood.

[opposite]
With its beautiful Regency profile, the table top sits on a fluted column and raised three-footed base. Between each panel of the table's frieze are roundels in ebony, typical of the Regency period.

[left]
This hall console table in an apartment in Kensington is made in santos rosewood, its curved scrolls terminating in roundels of turned bone. The Regency ethos is captured in the strong sense of formal symmetry. The gentle curve of the frieze is closed off at both ends by rectangular blocks.

[opposite]
To create a greater sense of lightness, the back panel is made from a single piece of white gold-leafed verre églomisé, which reflects the supporting scrolls. The interior of this Kensington apartment is by Justin Van Breda.

[following pages]
The design of the dining room of a Queen Anne house in London was based around the antique Regency table and chairs. Working with the architect Ian Adam-Smith, Gosling took the carved lion's head that features in the chair backs as a starting point and based its work around the Regency designer Thomas Hope. The mahogany cabinet to the left conceals a dumb waiter connected to the kitchen below and has a central mirrored section to reflect the listed panelling on the opposite wall.

[left and below right]
To stand against the listed Georgian panelling of the dining room, Gosling created a pair of tall mahogany plinths topped with urns and mirrored panels. The half urns are lit internally and project a warm light onto the verre églomisé panels above. These mirrors are 'scribed' onto the room's panels so as not to damage the listed fabric.

[below left]
The console table is supported by four hand-carved monopod lions that rest on a deep base plinth and an inset cantilevered top. The detailing of the legs can be found in Thomas Hope's *Household Furniture and Interior Decoration* (1807). The interior decoration is by Patti Money-Coutts.

[opposite]
A Regency dining chair with an exquisite hand-carved lion's head set into a roundel. The motif is echoed in the room's console table and large mahogany cabinet.

[preceding pages]
A powder room in black lacquerwork for the Queen Anne house in London. The wall designs are based on *A Treatise of Japanning and Varnishing* (1688) and were executed by DKT in London.

[below]
A deep serpentine entrance hall table in full-grained rosewood, made for a house in London. The gently curved scroll brackets appear almost to hold back the profile of the front frieze.

[opposite]
A circular walnut table based on Regency proportions, supported by a tapered and fluted column on a four-pointed base, made for a house in London. The chairs, also in walnut, are a classic shape designed by Gosling, with a distinctive central button in the upholstery just above table height.

[opposite and right]
This cabinet in English brown oak was created for a Regency country house. The roundels on the glazing bars attach the glass to the doors' framework and are typical of the Regency period.

[below]
A circular table in American walnut
designed in collaboration with Korner
Interiors, who also created the
contemporary setting. The table sits
on a wide scalloped base. The dramatic
scroll and carved legs are influenced by
Regency design and elements of a table
by Bill Blass in his New York apartment.

[opposite and following pages]
Details of the same circular table.
The table top has a deep banding of ebony
that encloses the beautifully bookmatched
burr oak centre.

[left and opposite]
An extraordinary English sycamore cabinet with hand-wrapped and -shaped vellum lozenges made for a Regency house in Kensington. The vellum-work, created by Rook's Books, is balanced on both sides to counter the pull of the skin as it shrinks. The dining table and chairs are made in mahogany by Gosling, while the interior design is by Judy Longbrook of JS Designs.

[following pages]
The desk, bookcase, bedhead and bedside tables of a Regency house in Kensington, designed for JS Designs. All are made in a beautiful santos rosewood with inlays of polished nickel. The use of different grain directions within a single pieces adds visual excitement.

A very graceful cabinet made in English
sycamore with bone handles and
a satinwood coloured carved base
and legs. It sits next to an antique
grisaille-painted and gilded Regency
klismos chair. Interior design of this
French château was by Todhunter Earle.

[opposite and right]
An octagonal games table with
a mirrored base designed for a French
château for Todhunter Earle. The table
is in walnut with bandings of ebony.
It occupies an octagonal room and
is accompanied by gilded Regency
chairs upholstered in purple silk velvet.

[opposite and below]
The games table for this French château contains a panel that has a sycamore and rosewood chessboard on one side and a green baize surface for card-playing on the other. Underneath the table top is a recessed backgammon board, also made from English sycamore and rosewood. All the pieces for both board games are hand-weighted.

[following pages]
An English ripple sycamore writing desk designed for a Todhunter Earle interior of a French château. The simple chamfered bronze edging belies the complexity of mitering the bronze around the frieze on each side. The legs are capped with bronze collars and finish in raised turned-bronze feet. The central writing surface is a blind-embossed leather panel dyed to match the colour of the sycamore exactly.

Victorian
1837–1900

THE DESIGN RULES

· Unadorned wood: gilding and other fancy finishes implied the hiding of shoddy workmanship ·
· Mixed materials such as ceramic plaques, metals, inlays of exotic woods · Applied decoration, including painted designs ·
· 'Revealed construction': a celebration of details such as pegged joints · Gothic and vernacular as alternatives to the
Neoclassical style · Use of native British woods · Elaboration of surfaces with inlays of silver, pewter and brass ·
Boulle work, mother-of-pearl, pietra dura, penwork and engraved ivory

MATERIALS

Early Victorian

Mahogany, burr walnut, birch, flame mahogany
and dyed veneers
Inlays of brass, ivory and bone stringing, boulle work
Marble and alabaster slabs, gilt-bronze mounts,
porcelain appliqués
Papier mâché, tortoiseshell, mother-of-pearl,
verre églomisé
Cast iron

Later Victorian

Native British woods: oak, elm, yew and walnut
Painted decoration
Ebonized beech with gilt accents
Inlays of historic materials: pewter, ivory, shell
Hinges, lock-plates and embellishments of beaten copper
Hand-worked pewter, silver, copper, enamelling
Natural fabrics and naturally derived dyes
Bamboo, cane, Japanese matting

LEADING FIGURES

Sir Charles Barry
[1795–1860]

Architect equally at home with Gothic and
classical styles. His most famous buildings were
the Gothic Palace of Westminster (in
collaboration with Pugin) and Highclere Castle,
but many of his country houses, such as
Cliveden, emulated the look of Italian palazzi.

Sir Joseph Paxton
[1803–1865]

Engineer. His early projects for the Duke of
Devonshire's estate at Chatsworth included the
construction of extraordinary fountains and
waterworks, and a vast greenhouse, the Great
Conservatory, which gave him the experience
necessary to conceive and execute the Crystal
Palace, the steel and glass structure that housed
the Great Exhibition of 1851.

Sir George Gilbert Scott
[1811–1878]

Architectural polymath. His Gothic buildings
include St Pancras Station, the Albert Memorial
and the heavy-handed restoration of Westminster
Abbey. His Foreign and Commonwealth Offices
in Whitehall showed him equally at home with
the Italianate classical style.

A. W. N. Pugin
[1812–1852]

Architect and apologist of the true Gothic style.
His churches and domestic buildings sought to
revive the glory of the Catholic Middle Ages. In
addition to his decorative schemes for the Palace
of Westminster, his designs for usable Gothic
furniture were innovative and influential.

Philip Webb
[1831–1915]

Architect and furniture designer. Webb trained
with the Gothic Revival architect G. E. Street.
His design for William Morris's Red House,
blending medieval and vernacular elements, was a
crucial forerunner of the Arts and Crafts style.

E. W. Godwin
[1833–1886]

Architect and designer of furniture, fabrics and
wallpapers. He abandoned the heaviness and
revealed construction of the Gothic style for the
delicacy of Japanese models. His decorative
collaborations with Whistler were central to the
evolution of the Aesthetic Movement.

William Morris
[1834–1896]

Poet, designer, craftsman, conservationist and
early socialist. Morris's extraordinary energy
allowed him to master many different crafts in a
wide range of materials. His advocacy of fine
natural materials and joyous handwork made him
the father of the Arts and Crafts Movement. He
ran an influential firm, Morris and Co., and his
idealistic socialism and concern for the
preservation of ancient buildings also made him a
prophetic thinker.

C. F. A. Voysey
[1857–1941]

Architect and designer of furniture, fabrics,
wallpaper and metalwork. Though a major
proponent of the Arts and Crafts style, Voysey
did not despise the use of commercial
manufacturing processes if the materials were fine
and the resulting goods of high quality. His
architectural style was much copied, to the
ultimate detriment of his reputation.

Charles Rennie Mackintosh
[1868–1928]

Architect and designer, leader of the close-knit
Glasgow School, idiosyncratic adherents of the
Arts and Crafts Movement. His designs for his
masterpiece, the Glasgow School of Art, gained
him an international reputation, but when he
moved south and adopted a more modernist style
his career faltered. In later years he abandoned
architectural practice and became a painter.

[page 84]
Detail of the brown oak library installed
in an Arts and Crafts country house (see
page 100). Brown oak is in fact the
result of a fungus, *Fistunlina hepatica*,
which creates the rich brown colouring.
The hand-dovetailed doors have ebony
handles and brass grillework finely
shaped into overlapping elliptic forms.

The very long reign of Queen Victoria coincided with one of the most extraordinary and colourful eras of British art and design. It was also one of the most diverse, for the simple description 'Victorian' can embrace every type of furniture and decoration from the elegant, still Neoclassical taste of the queen's youth in the 1830s through to the enthusiasm for historicizing design and overwhelming ornamentation that characterized the vast majority of the pieces shown in the Great Exhibition of 1851. Then, in the 1860s, we can trace the beginnings of the artistic repugnance to that riot of machine-made opulence – a reaction that gave rise to the Aesthetic Movement of the 1870s and the Arts and Crafts Movement, but also, at the end of the century, to the wilder excesses of Art Nouveau and even the first glimmerings of modernism. Clearly some more precise signposts are required if we are to negotiate the wildly changing fashions of these seven eventful and innovative decades.

As we have seen, fashions do not change in precise step with the accessions or deaths of kings and queens. When the young Victoria ascended the throne in 1837, the styles of furniture popular in the days of her uncles George IV and William IV evolved only gradually. Classical forms prevailed for a while at least, and mahogany remained the most usual wood for everyday furniture, even if, at the upper end of the market, more exotically grained burr woods and pale veneers enjoyed a certain fashionable cachet. What we see in the first decade of the young queen's reign is a progressive tendency towards heavier construction and a more emphatic use of ornament. Except in the most grandiose furnishings of palaces and mansions, Regency carving had tended towards the light and delicate, matching the general delicacy of the pieces themselves. By the 1840s embellishments appear far more solid. Bolder

curlicues and massive lion's-paw feet adorn the bases of tables, while fleshy acanthus leaves, anthemions (stylized honeysuckle flowers) and solid motifs such as the acroterion (the corner ornament of a pediment) proliferate, often picked out with gilding. The emergence of this weighty, late Neoclassicism in both furniture and architecture coincides with the development of Victorian industry and machine culture, and, curiously, seems to match the confident energy of the new railway age.

Old-fashioned connoisseurs once held it as an article of faith that 'good taste stopped in 1837', and it is certainly true that, by the later 1840s, the process was far advanced whereby newer and often ungainly types of furniture had all but replaced the lightness and delicacy of Regency pieces. For example, the classic dining chair of the 1820s – ancient Greek in inspiration, poised on slender sabre legs and usually fitted with a caned seat supporting a thin squab cushion – had been supplanted by the squat balloon-back chair, with its disproportionately deep, but admittedly more comfortable, padded seat. Similarly, the increasingly cluttered drawing room of the well-to-do middle-class home now boasted a welcoming array of deeply buttoned, sprung-upholstered sofas and chairs in place of the previous austerity of a horsehair-covered Grecian couch.

In architectural terms, too, this was a period of radical change. As with furniture, the classical architecture of the day evolved, becoming richer and heavier and taking inspiration from Renaissance Italianate sources as much as from the pure styles of antiquity. But this was also a time of more fundamental oppositions. The so-called 'Battle of the Styles', an ideological conflict fought out in print as much as in brick and stone, pitted the supporters of classical orthodoxy against the enthusiasm of the Gothic Revivalists led by A. W. N. Pugin.

The controversy centred on more than mere aesthetic
differences: the Establishment promoted classicism as the style
of civilization and authority; the Goths claimed that, in Pugin's
memorable phrase, 'true Christian or pointed architecture' held
the moral and religious high ground and, moreover, could
claim to be the legacy of a more ancient British culture. Each
side had its victories: after much heated argument, the Houses
of Parliament were built in a 'patriotic' Gothic style by Sir
Charles Barry (but with all the detail supplied by Pugin), while,
for the design of Sir George Gilbert Scott's new Foreign and
Commonwealth Offices on Whitehall, the powers within
government dictated that it should be classical. It should
perhaps be added as a footnote that, with the exception of
the hard-line, unflinchingly Catholic Gothicism of Pugin,
most of the major architects of the day were happy to reach
an entirely pragmatic accommodation with their clients as to
which style they should adopt for lucrative commissions.

For their masterful, intricate detailing, Pugin's interiors
are fascinating. Having in his youth drawn many designs for
frivolous Regency Gothick pieces, Pugin studiously researched
original medieval examples and in his mature years evolved a
new kind of furniture based on the strong, simple qualities of
ancient carpenters' work. His reverence for plain English oak
and the principle of 'revealed construction' led him to favour
stoutly pegged mortice joints and to avoid the use of all the
'dishonest' methods prevalent in the commercial furniture
trade, which cosmeticized poor materials and passed off shoddy
workmanship under layers of French polish. One unexpected
outcome of Pugin's realization that his furniture could be sent
from the workshop to customers by train in separate pieces,
ready to be assembled on arrival, is that he is now seen as the
progenitor of the flat-pack revolution.

Technological innovation lay at the heart of the Great
Exhibition of 1851. This vauntingly ambitious undertaking was
undoubtedly the most significant episode that had ever taken
place in the history of design. The show – or, to give it its full
title, 'The Great Exhibition of the Works of Industry of all
Nations' – was held in Hyde Park, London, in a ground-
breaking building that came to be known, for obvious reasons,
as the Crystal Palace. Designed by a brilliant young architect-
engineer of garden hothouses, Joseph Paxton, the vast steel and
glass structure – almost one-third of a mile long and large
enough to enclose mature trees in the park – was erected in
record time owing to the novel use of prefabrication for the
columns and enormous curved beams that spanned the width
of the nave. As a further brilliant innovation, the 300,000 panes
of glass needed to complete the structure were installed by
multiple teams of glaziers who worked from wheeled wagons
running along the intricate web of cast-iron rainwater gutters
that criss-crossed the building 30 metres (100 feet) above the
ground. Two thousand workmen completed the building in
just eight months.

Conceived by a team of bureaucrats led by Albert, the
Prince Consort, and Sir Henry Cole (later director of the
South Kensington Museum), the spectacular show opened
on time, on budget and ran smoothly for a year. In that time
almost 8 million visitors viewed the unfeasibly enormous
number of exhibits, which included industrial objects ranging
from steam engines to teaspoons, agricultural products and
examples of traditional craft, ethnographic material and
modern factory-made household items by the thousands.
Contemporary painting and sculpture also figured, though their
relevant sections were modest by comparison with the range
and richness of the applied and decorative art displays, which

[below]
A rare and rather splendid peepshow,
designed by George Bragg and published
by W. Spooner of London, showing the
Great Exhibition of 1851.

[opposite]
During construction of the Crystal
Palace, wheeled wagons that ran along
the gutters enabled glaziers to work
on the building's vast roof.

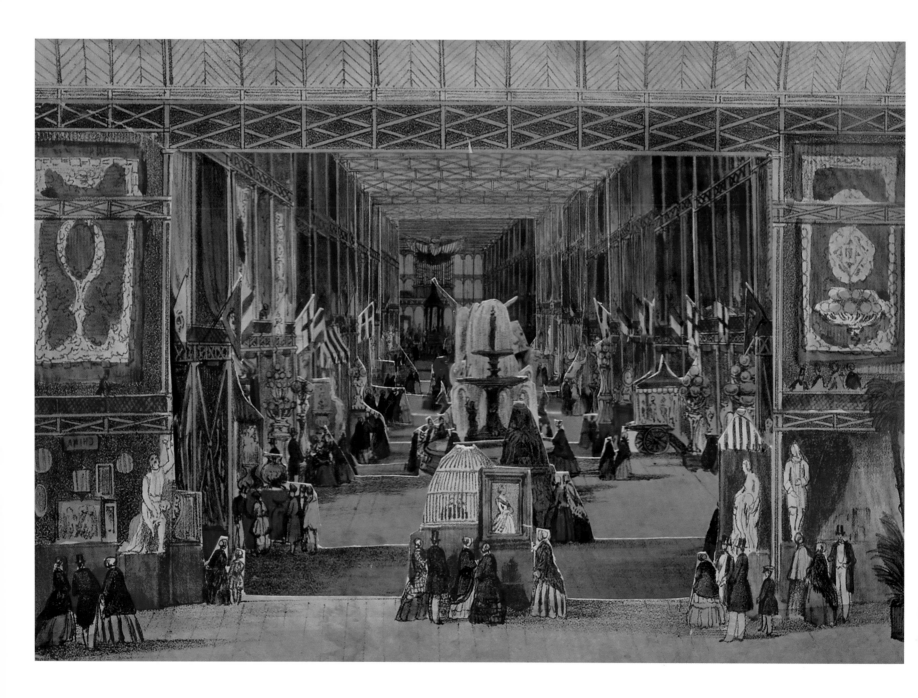

offered the cream of furniture, metalwork, ceramics, textiles and other ornamental goods of the day. A notable aspect of the furniture exhibits was the large number that involved the use of novel materials in their manufacture. Besides those made in wood, both native and exotic, pieces created from cast or wrought iron, cane, leather, composite stone and even papier mâché could also be seen. Papier-mâché pieces finished in black lacquer and ornamented with painted decoration and mother-of-pearl inlays enjoyed a particular, if short-lived, vogue during these years.

The other most conspicuous characteristic of a high proportion of the objects of applied and decorative art in the show was the extent to which their makers seemed to rely on a large scale and a plethora of ornament – often created by casting from moulds or by machine-carving – in order to render their pieces noticeable and, as they thought, more praiseworthy and saleable. Many furniture-makers, for example, chose to show 'exhibition pieces' far too large for any ordinary domestic context and often laden with ornamental metalwork, over-elaborate inlays and other elements such as inset porcelain plaques in the French eighteenth-century manner. Such pieces, encouraging a vulgar, overwrought attempt to create eye-catching luxury goods, inevitably had a deleterious effect on the general trade practice of the day, and led to the wholesale encrusting of everyday things in meretricious historicizing ornament.

Even at the time, critical voices were raised to challenge the preconception that piling on the ornament was a virtue. Indeed, one of the key official publications, the *Report to the Juries*, warned in its guidelines for judging the merit of exhibits in the decoration and furnishings sections that: 'It is not necessary that an object be covered with ornament; or extravagant in

form, to obtain the element of beauty; articles of furniture are too often crowded with unnecessary embellishment which, besides adding to their cost, interferes with their use.' This statement, in a nutshell, frames the philosophical and aesthetic questions that would dominate the debate concerning the nature and true purpose of design for the rest of the nineteenth century – a debate that continued with renewed vehemence into the twentieth century and still troubles our own age.

Perhaps the most significant rethink – not just about style in furniture, but about the very nature of furnishings and how they are created – came in the mid-1850s as the result of William Morris and his friend Edward Burne-Jones taking over a set of bare rooms once occupied by their mentor, the Pre-Raphaelite painter-poet Dante Gabriel Rossetti. Needing furniture but finding nothing to suit their romanticized longing for the Middle Ages, they began to fashion some heavy, rather crudely constructed chairs and tables, which they painted with figures from medieval tales and bold, bright patterns derived from ancient decoration. Some more sophisticated tables and cabinets resulted when Morris's architect friend Philip Webb joined them and designed several pieces to be made in the carpentry workshops of a nearby boys' home. Webb's ingenious reworking and melding of medieval and simple vernacular chimed perfectly with the bold painted decoration carried out by Burne-Jones and other friends. The finest of these pieces, such as the St George Cabinet, now in the Victoria and Albert Museum, London, are very close in feel to the experiments in painted medieval-style furniture created around this time by another close associate of the group, the Gothic Revival architect William Burges.

When Morris and his beautiful wife, Janey, moved into the Red House at Bexleyheath, designed for them by Webb in

a sort of medieval vernacular style, the idea of making his own embroidered hangings, wallpapers, tiles and painted decoration seized the energetic Morris. He came to the realization that, in order to have a house in which the interiors were artistic, poetic and constructed from good materials with joy in the making, it would be necessary to master each of the manufacturing processes in turn and to reinvent them thoroughly, going back to the first principles as he found them in the Middle Ages. In 1861, with this simple but hugely ambitious aim, Morris, supported by the design skills of his painter friends, founded his celebrated firm of 'art workmen'.

At the big international exhibition held in South Kensington in 1862, a new spirit of 'design reform' had raised the general level of exhibits considerably. Morris's firm made a strong showing and rapidly gained acclaim for its stained glass as well as a growing range of domestic furnishings. Over time, in addition to wallpaper-making Morris would master the intricacies of printing and weaving fabrics, the preparing of yarns with natural dyes, tapestry-weaving, calligraphy, wood-engraving and hand-press printing. When Morris died in 1896, his doctor gave the cause of death as 'simply being William Morris, and having done the work of ten men'.

At the heart of all Morris's activities lay his genius for pattern design; this was based always on his love of nature and deep knowledge of plants. His deep belief that the salvation of society lay in a rediscovery of the value of craftsmanship and 'honest work' led him in his later years to embrace an idealistic form of socialism – another cause to which he devoted huge energy. At the same time Morris's deep concern for the historic fabric of England made him a proto-conservationist and led him to become a founder of the Society for the Protection of Historic Buildings.

In his own mind Morris never reconciled the problem that his wares, beautifully crafted from the best materials, were necessarily expensive to produce and thus beyond the means of the ordinary workman looking to furnish his house. Only the well-known Morris & Co. 'Sussex' chair and other simple, inexpensive pieces of furniture ever reached a wide market but, nevertheless, Morris's example had far-reaching consequences for the development of design and decoration during the rest of Victoria's reign. Furthermore, his ideas inspired two movements that, if not entirely irreconcilable, were certainly quite different in their motivation and aims: the Aesthetic Movement and the Arts and Crafts Movement.

The Aesthetic Movement, which flourished in the 1870s, sought to bring about a quiet revolution in art and decoration and to create a new 'cult of beauty'. Allied to earlier attempts at design reform and uniting aspects of both the Pre-Raphaelite attitude to medievalism and the classicism of painters such as Lord Leighton, Aestheticism engendered a hybrid style that was deliberately recherché and that appealed to the languid and self-consciously precious. Aesthetic taste was also remarkably eclectic, and the interiors created by the Aesthetes included a rich mix of objects, which might embrace old blue-and-white china and Middle Eastern ceramics, old carved furniture, sleek new ebonized chairs and cabinets, and sumptuous curtains and carpets.

The idea of buying antique or old and decorative furniture and using it in a domestic context was something of an innovation. Rossetti is usually credited with having been among the first to see the visual and associative qualities of such pieces. When he moved into an old, dark Queen Anne house next to the river in Chelsea in 1862, it is recorded that he trawled the junk shops of South London and the sailors'

pawn-shops of the East End searching out four-poster beds and
tattered crewel-work curtains, dim looking-glasses, lacquer
cabinets and other curiosities. According to the Aesthetic creed,
when all these disparate things were selected with the eye of an
artist they could be welded into a harmonious arrangement in
which colour and pattern united them. As Oscar Wilde, the
self-appointed prophet of Aestheticism, proclaimed:
'All beautiful things belong to the same age.'

The finest furniture made for Aesthetic interiors were the
creations of the architect E. W. Godwin, who worked often
in collaboration with his friend the painter James McNeill
Whistler. Godwin had begun his career as a devotee of the
Gothic, designing immensely heavy, throne-like chairs, but his
discovery of the inventive qualities of Chinese architectural
woodwork and the delicacy of Japanese crafts, combined with
his study of surviving examples of Egyptian and ancient Greek
furniture, all conspired to transform his vision utterly. His
Aesthetic pieces, such as his famous – and much-copied – small
occasional table is a masterpiece of lightness and understated
elegance.

Although Morris loved a profusion of pattern and also
filled his rooms with pretty objects – mixing such things as
Indian bronze peacocks and sixteenth-century Iznik dishes with
his tapestries and ancient oak coffers – his attitude to furnishing
remained in some ways essentially austere. 'Have nothing in
your house,' he wrote, 'that you do not know to be useful, or
believe to be beautiful.' In one sense this fine maxim brings him
close to the dispels of Aestheticism, but it is also a foundation
text for that other great movement, the Arts and Crafts.

Taking a lead from Morris's ideal of fine craftsmanship and
the employment of nothing but the finest of materials, a whole
school of furniture designers and makers of other household

wares sought to rediscover the simplicity of earlier times and to embrace the joy of making good things in a pleasant workshop surrounding. Consciously modelling themselves on a highly romanticized notion of the Middle Ages, furniture-makers shaped oak and other timbers into traditional forms, leaving the beauty of the wood unadorned or embellishing it with simple inlays inspired by natural forms. This was a rural ideal, and the greatest concentration of such workshops were – and perhaps still are – to be found in the West Country, in the stretch of largely unspoiled England that lies beyond William Morris's beloved old Cotswold manor house at Kelmscott.

It is perhaps entirely characteristic of a century in which a restless search for new styles, for experiment and for innovation in architecture, decoration and design had been the order of the day that the final decade of the queen's long reign would see a hectic succession of new ideas. Though never entirely embraced in the United Kingdom, the European Art Nouveau style found a certain degree of acceptance, even if an old guard of designers including Morris's ally Walter Crane fulminated against it. When the Victoria and Albert Museum in London acquired some startling pieces of Art Nouveau furniture from the Paris 1900 exhibition, Crane and others protested that their display posed a threat to the taste and even the morals of honest British craftsmen, insisting that these dangerous pieces should be banished from the museum's galleries.

The emergence of a somewhat less obviously foreign style, home-grown but in no sense less innovative, is epitomized by the work of two architects and designers whose careers crossed from the Victorian age into the twentieth century: C. F. A. Voysey and Charles Rennie Mackintosh. As a designer of furniture, Voysey seems to take his lead from the best of the

Arts and Crafts ideals but adds distinctive flourishes of his own. A plain oak bureau will be enlivened by extravagant beaten-copper hinges and an exquisitely fretted lock plate; what appears at first glance to be a countrified ladder-back chair reveals the addition of extra slats to enhance the height of the back, and a refinement of detail that lifts it above the average cottage piece. While Voysey's architecture has a similar, subtly subversive stance that plays with both vernacular and more obviously 'modern' elements, its qualities can be harder to appreciate. This is for the unfortunate reason that so many of Voysey's best ideas for domestic buildings, and even his small stylistic traits, were copied and traduced by the builders of the vast swathes of suburban ribbon-development semi-detached housing that spread unstoppably across Home Counties England in the inter-war years.

By contrast, Mackintosh's highly idiosyncratic, sublime, rectilinear Art Nouveau found few imitators, and his reputation as an innovator has stood the test of time. His furniture designs, which include several versions of an iconic, extravagantly high-backed chair – originally designed for Miss Cranston's Glasgow tea rooms – stand comparison with the most striking pieces of any of his continental rivals. Though never fully appreciated in his native Scotland or in England, Mackintosh's greatest buildings – such the Glasgow School of Art, tragically damaged by fire in 2014 – secured him a very high reputation in Germany and elsewhere in Europe. This note of internationalism forms a fitting point to conclude an account of the Victorian era, the last period in which the story of artistic, architectural and cultural development is still largely a national one. Henceforth, architecture, design and ideas will recognize no such boundaries.

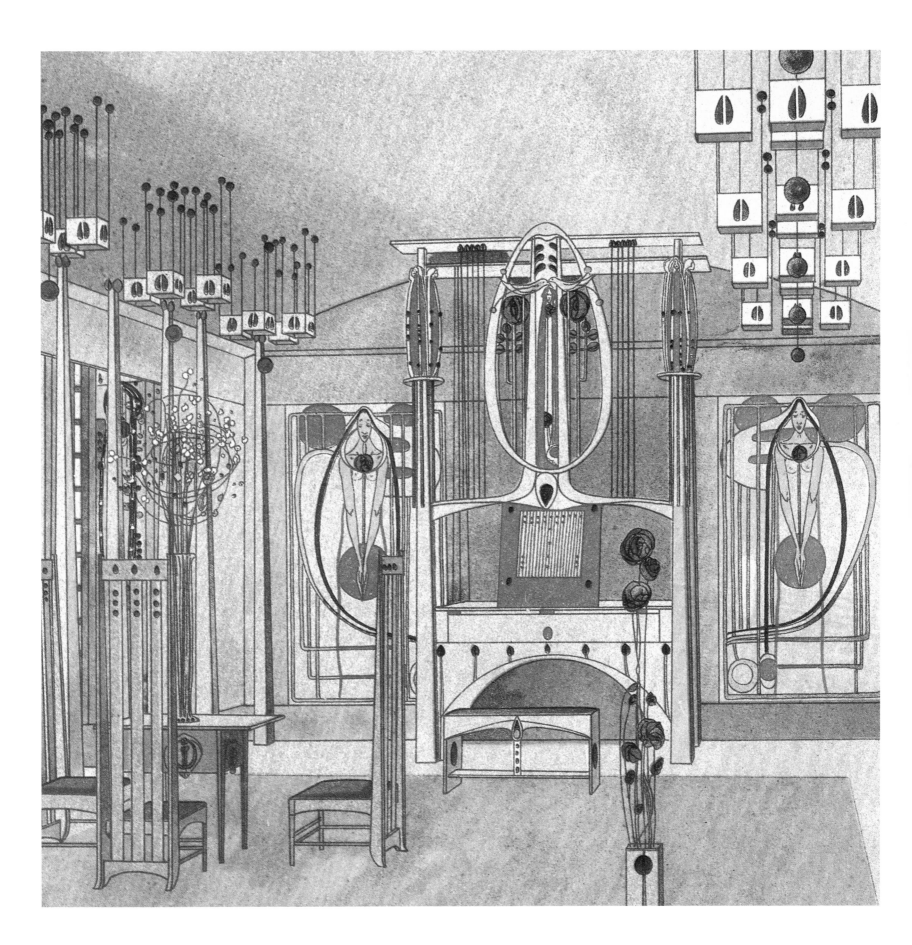

An expanding circular table and bookcases in vellum and limed oak for a London apartment designed by Lavinia Dargie. The Victorian corbel arch is mirrored in the table's scroll legs. The bookcases are inset with vellum-wrapped lozenge panels at top and bottom, creating a link with the console table on the right.

[opposite]

Detail of the circular expanding table illustrated on the previous pages. The top is covered in over seventy-eight panels of dark brown shagreen (here a type of ray skin). The skin of the male ray has a distinctive 'eye' marking, which here is oriented towards the centre of the table top.

[right]

Six triangular sections can be pulled away from the centre to reveal folding leaves stored inside the table top, which serve to expand the table's surface area. All these panels are edged with solid Indian ebony. The legs are hand-carved in sycamore and inlaid with macassar ebony. A brass ring locks them together for added stability.

[above]
The detailing of an Arts and Crafts library designed for a fifteenth-century country house. The library furniture is made in brown oak with square 'pegs' of Indian ebony. The shape of the mouldings is based on the house's original medieval ceiling beams.

[right]
The library was designed to house a collection of first-day cover stamp albums, which are stored behind doors fitted with hand-worked elliptical grills and contrasting panels in English ripple sycamore. The desk has ebony feet and handles, and follows the Arts and Crafts motif of 'pegging' in the corner posts.

[opposite]

A pair of games tables in mahogany were made for this wonderful barrel-vaulted Arts and Crafts room in an English country house. They were designed by Gosling for long weekend games of roulette, cards, backgammon, scrabble and chess. The interior was designed by Patti Money-Coutts and architect Ian Adam-Smith.

[left and below]

At the corners of each table, and halfway along the frieze, are hand-carved medallions whose design is taken from the rosettes on the Victorian arched minstrels gallery. The bases of the games tables are Victorian in essence and support hand-carved knop columns. These styling details all have their origins in the Elizabethan period but were reinterpreted by the romanticized storytelling of the Aesthetic Movement.

[preceding pages and above]
A set of bookcases in brown oak and dark-stained English oak created for the study of an important Victorian country house. The castellations are taken from the door pediments, and the arches from the ceiling's plasterwork and the original hall panelling. The restoration of the house – designed originally by G. E. Street, the architect best known for his Gothic-style Law Courts on the Strand, London – was overseen by Ian Adam-Smith, with interior design by Victoria Fairfax.

[right]
The dressing room of the same house, created by Gosling in collaboration with Victoria Fairfax. The room's design is that of a jewel box, and it is made from the most exceptional materials – verre églomisé panels, mother-of-pearl, shagreen hand-dyed a special denim blue – set into a framework of English oak.

[opposite]
The dressing table has a frieze of shagreen and mother-of-pearl, with hand-blown and cut-crystal handles. The lower drawer section is designed in quartered-cut verre églomisé panels.

[preceding pages]
The asymmetrical Victorian entrance hall was designed by Street in 1873 to look as if it had grown up over a period of time. The wish to create an 'instant' historical story was prevalent within the Aesthetic Movement.

[left]
Detail of the brown oak cabinets Gosling designed for the study. The central block and radiating sections of raised panels can be found on the house's original door detailing.

Art Moderne
and Art Deco
1910–1939

THE DESIGN RULES

· The 'Rule of Three', in which design elements are split into three parts: three panels, three lines, three juxtaposed materials ·
· A sense of symmetry ·
· A backdrop of subtle curves ·
· Zig-zag lightning bolts and straight parallel lines ·
· Use of rare and exotic materials ·

MATERIALS

Macassar ebony, rosewood
Ivory and bone stringing and inlays
Tortoiseshell, mother-of-pearl, verre églomisé
Marquetry, straw-work,
Black lacquer, vellum, parchment, plywood
Bronze, silver, nickel

LEADING FIGURES

Roger Fry
[1866–1934]
Painter, connoisseur and art critic, leading figure of the Bloomsbury Group. Fry championed modern art in England and coined the term 'Post-Impressionist'. In 1913 he founded the Omega Workshops with the aim of creating furnishings with a modern painterly aesthetic.

Jean Dunand
[1877–1947]
Decorative painter and designer. Swiss-born and originally trained as a sculptor, Dunand was one of the most accomplished craftsmen of the Deco period. He worked in copper and other metals. Under the instruction of Seizo Sugawara, Dunand also revived the art of true lacquerwork in the Japanese manner.

Paul Poiret
[1879–1944]
At the height of his fame as one of the leading Parisian couturiers, in 1911 Poiret added an interior decoration and furnishing business to his activities. Capitalizing on the link between fashion and decoration, the Atelier Martine was the prototype for many such small, chic firms.

Jacques-Émile Ruhlmann
[1879–1933]
Ruhlmann's Alsatian family ran a conventional decorating firm, which he took over on his father's death in 1907. He established himself as a designer of furniture in exotic materials and by the time of the Paris 1925 exhibition was regarded as the leading exponent of Art Deco.

Armand-Albert Rateau
[1882–1938]
At the age of 23, Rateau became the director of the prestigious Paris decorating firm Maison Alavoine but set up his own business in 1919. His bronze cast furniture became the most important expression of his classically inspired style, but by the late 1920s he employed over 200 craftsmen working in all materials.

André Groult
[1884–1967]
Furniture designer and interior decorator. His furniture was inspired by organic forms and made with rare and exquisite materials. His surrealist shagreen-covered chest of drawers, known as the *Chiffonnier Antrophomorphe* (1925), is perhaps the most celebrated piece of Art Deco furniture.

Jean-Michel Frank
[1895–1941]
Interior decorator. Frank's early mentors were Sergei Diaghilev, whom he met in Venice, and the taste-maker Madame Eugenia Errazuriz, who guided him towards chic minimalism and a love of good materials. Much of his best work was carried out during his partnership with Adolphe Chanaux between 1930 and 1939.

André-Léon Arbus
[1903–1969]
An architect, designer and interior decorator, Arbus based much of his furniture on classical or French Empire period models, but gave it a scale and powerful presence that belonged to the Deco period. His bold, simplified upholstery forms have remained influential.

Among old-fashioned antique dealers there used to be a saying to the effect that if a good-looking French Louis XV or Louis XVI commode was finely finished at the back and had drawers that ran smoothly and effortlessly, then the piece was undoubtedly a fake. The old *ébénistes*, it was argued, were quite happy to use rough wood where it did not show, whereas those who purchased the versions produced by late nineteenth-century furnishing firms demanded their money's worth in terms of finish. This tells us a great deal about the taste of the times, for, as we have seen, the nineteenth-century love of the past meant that much of the furnishing and decoration carried out between the 1830s and 1900 was in historical styles.

Aesthetic, Arts and Crafts, Art Nouveau and proto-modernist furniture and interiors were always embraced enthusiastically by an avant-garde minority. Well into the twentieth century, most people were more comfortable with surroundings that were 'traditional'; as a result, much of the furnishing trade was employed in making pieces in the styles of the past at every level of the market, from the manufacture of everyday household furniture to the creation of upmarket pastiches, high-quality copies and outright fakes. This is an observation easily confirmed by a glance at the trade catalogues and popular decoration magazines of the period, or by a visit to any provincial auction house today – either in the United Kingdom, where mock-Tudor, neo-Georgian and Regency Revival pieces will usually outnumber the genuine article, or in France, where the supply of bogus Louis XV and Louis XVI 'meubles de style' still seems endless.

Fortunately, such conservative conformism was never the whole story, and the demand for new, fashionable furnishings in contemporary styles was, while never large, at least sufficient to stimulate invention and to support a number of talented designers and craftsmen, especially in France. In the early decades of the twentieth century, Paris – the city that had long enjoyed its unassailable reputation as the centre of couture and fashion – now gained an equal ascendancy as the world's art capital. Music, theatre, painting and sculpture all flourished, and the avant-garde literary scene that had its origins in Parisian intellectual café life became increasingly international, with British, American and Russian artists and writers adding to the melting pot of ideas. In his hothouse climate, design reflected the renewed energy of the fine arts, and decoration was touched by the influence of a succession of exciting new art movements, such as Cubism and Fauvism, that emerged in the years immediately before and after the First World War.

Within this vibrant world of design, we can certainly discern two distinct and very different tendencies. One, promoted principally by architects and a new breed of product designers, was towards an uncompromising vision that turned its back on the past in the search for new solutions and new lifestyles. This modernist viewpoint, and the international movement that began to coalesce at this time, is the subject of the next chapter. By contrast, the artists, furniture designers and interior decorators that we shall look at here, although no less inventive, viewed their work as a continuation of all that was finest in the past – as part, indeed, of a grand tradition stretching back to the great period of creativity and discerning patronage in the days of the *ancien régime*. They were inspired by the achievements of the great furniture-makers of the eighteenth and nineteenth centuries and – in a way that, as a designer working a century later, I hope to follow – sought to create new decorative styles that reflected that tradition but belonged wholly to the new age.

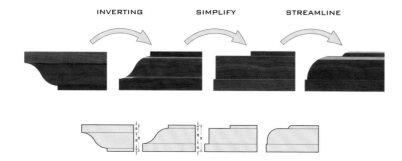

INVERTING   SIMPLIFY   STREAMLINE

[left]
A Gosling illustration created to show how a classical ogee moulding can be inverted and squared up to become an Art Deco step. In the final drawing, the step receives an additional curve, taking it into the 'Streamlined Moderne' style.

[opposite]
A bathroom designed by Armand-Albert Rateau for the Duchess of Alba's Liria Palace, Madrid. The exceptional and almost naive painting style was used as inspiration for the verre églomisé panels on pages 124–25.

Following the end of the Great War, a new attitude not just to decoration but to life in general became apparent. No doubt as a deliberate contrast to the horrors and privations of the war, Paris and London in the Twenties embraced pleasure, frivolity and luxury, but it was in Paris especially that the dual notions of *grand luxe* and *chic* were formed and flourished. In some ways the figure who most perfectly exemplifies this milieu is Paul Poiret. Celebrated as a couturier whose creations embraced influences as diverse as chaste Neoclassical dresses and the most decadently exuberant Arabian Nights fantasies, Poiret was also an influential designer of interiors. Through his Atelier Martine, one of the earliest of the brilliant small-scale, esoteric and exclusive decorating studios, Poiret realized his vision of the private interior as a place of luxury and fantasy. His speciality was the creation of sumptuous furnishings in which lavish Russian Ballet-style draperies, tasselled cushions of richly coloured satins and tactile silk velvets played a significant part. With the sure eye of the polished couturier, he fearlessly mixed patterns ranging from eighteenth-century brocades and Turkish 'bizarre' florals, through to the latest Cubist-inspired 'jazz-modern' fabrics designed by friends including the painter Raoul Dufy.

One of Poiret's most publicized successes was his decoration of the interiors of the barge *Amours*, which, moored on the Seine close to the show site, was his daring contribution to the international exhibition held in 1925. This *Exposition Internationale des Arts Décoratifs et Industriels Modernes* was a worthy successor to London's Great Exhibition of 1851 and the memorable Paris World's Fair of 1900. Gathering together, as those previous events had done, all that was most extraordinary – if not always most tasteful – in contemporary craftsmanship and manufactures, the 1925

show established the look of the age. The title, with its specific mention of the 'arts décoratifs', also led to the distinctively new style of decoration and design (which up until that point had been described only tentatively as 'art moderne') being identified henceforth as 'Art Deco'.

The view that the decorative arts in France, and French modern furniture design in particular, were at this date markedly superior to those of any rival nations seemed to be all too readily demonstrated by the very varied quality of contributions to the 1925 exhibition. It was sadly admitted at the time that the British – and indeed others – made a poor showing, submitting frankly dull rather than adventurous rooms and pieces of furniture largely in historic and traditional styles. By comparison, the offerings of the French designers and manufacturers looked not just more 'modern', but infinitely more sophisticated in terms of both taste and craftsmanship.

In general the English, having led the advance around the turn of the century, had been slow to come to terms with modernism. One of the few serious attempts in the years immediately before the First World War to imagine how new artistic ideas could be applied in the sphere of household furnishings had been the painter and art critic Roger Fry's Omega Workshops experiment. Fry had enlisted his Bloomsbury Group friends to create painted furniture, textiles and ceramics that reflected their regard for recent Post-Impressionist and Cubist French art. Sadly, Fry's vision of an avant-garde urban collective-cum-cottage industry did not succeed. Few among the Bloomsbury coterie of earnest painters and enthusiastic amateurs possessed the craft skills required to translate their pictorial ideas into actual everyday furnishings; the result was that the productions of the workshop, although

evidently created in a spirit of aesthetic excitement and jolly bohemian camaraderie, were often somewhat impractical and never sufficiently well made to attract a wider or more influential clientele.

By comparison with the homely wares offered by the Omega Workshops, the pieces made by the newly emerging Parisian ateliers of the 1920s were the height of quality and chic. Displaying craftsmanship at its finest, their best pieces rivalled the boldness of design of the seventeenth-century master André-Charles Boulle and the concern for finish of the great later eighteenth-century *ébénistes* such as Jean-Henri Riesener. Public interest was intense, and Art Deco became the style of grand private interiors, smart restaurants and hotels, and luxury ocean liners – such as the famous SS *Normandie* – and it was adopted by the designers of 'the movies' in the heyday of Hollywood glamour. Indeed, so great was the association between glamour and Art Deco that the makers of the new appurtenances of fashionable life – cars, aeroplanes, telephones and gramophones – all appropriated aspects of the style for their designs.

An intriguing feature of the 1925 exhibition was the degree of popular attention it received from an unprecedentedly wide public. One important contributory factor in this was the appearance of a very large number of official, semi-official and commercial publications that described the exhibits. One of the most revealing of these is a volume compiled by Léon Deshairs with the title *Intérieures en Couleurs* (Paris, 1925), which comprises a breathtaking array of illustrations showing many of the exhibition's set-piece furnished rooms. I find these images especially inspirational for the way in which they not only document the detail of individual pieces of furniture and their placing in the rooms, but also give a real sense of the luxurious atmosphere that designers such as Paul Poiret and Jacques-Émile Ruhlmann conjured in these temporary spaces.

As one of the leading furniture-makers and designers of interior schemes, Ruhlmann was accorded a prominent position within the exhibition site. Acting as an inspired impresario, Ruhlmann gathered around him a team that included the talented architect Pierre Patout, as well as several of the best decorative painters, sculptors and textile designers of the day.

The resulting showpiece, the Hôtel d'un Collectionneur, was conceived as the home of an imaginary contemporary Maecenas. It was a free-standing building in a modern classical architectural style that successfully married an excitingly new ziggurat form with the cool, clean lines of the best of eighteenth-century French garden pleasure pavilions. In contrast to much exhibition architecture, the chaste exterior was almost devoid of ornamentation, save for a rich bas-relief frieze by Joseph Barnard that adorned the elegantly curved window-bay of the structure's central space. This grandly scaled room was adorned with large decorative panels by Jean Dunand, rich carpets and other textiles, and several important pieces of furniture by Ruhlmann himself, including a superb *bonheur-du-jour*, or writing table, in ebony lacquer with contrasting white stringing in ivory. Beside this exquisite piece stood an en-suite chair poised on the most delicate curving legs. The Ruhlmann pavilion was, and still is, widely hailed as the very epitome of 1925 chic.

In Ruhlmann's work, as in that produced by many of the designers of the Deco period, I often discern an observance – whether conscious or not is hard to say – of a characteristic formula, whereby design elements such as decorative panels or lines of inlaid decoration are grouped in threes. This 'rule of three' seems characteristic of the style, and I often play with it when called upon to evoke the luxury and chic of the 1920s and 1930s in a new interior. In this respect Art Deco, which was the subject of an enthusiastic revival in the 1970s, has in some ways never ceased to be an enduring style statement. My own feeling, however, is that one should learn from the past but always restate the old themes in a contemporary idiom. To this end I have always sought to understand the essence of the work of designers I admire, never to copy it. This approach is true

especially of my interest in a number of the most important artists and designers of the Deco period, from whom one can learn so much about scale, proportion and, in particular, the use of fine materials.

Gilbert Poillerat was the master of the inventive use of metal in an idiosyncratic, neo-Baroque manner. For his instantly recognizable furniture, he contrived to bring the exuberance of French late seventeenth-century ironwork indoors, reworking characteristic motifs such as the 'S' shapes and curlicues of palace garden gates into the supports of monumental marble-topped tables and the backs and legs of chairs. Finishing his pieces with simple lacquered surfaces or enriching them further with discreet gilding, Poillerat extended the repertoire of Parisian furniture-making in a way that would continue to be popular well into the 1950s and 1960s. It was embraced not only in France, but also on the west coast of the United States, where the Baroque energy and highly decorative effect of wrought ironwork remained in vogue for a long time.

If Poillerat's furniture can be said to derive from the methods of ornamental ironwork, the metal pieces created by Armand-Albert Rateau reveal the eye and hand of a sculptor working within the tradition of highly finished bronze-casting. Ratteau introduced into his pieces a distinct note of imagination and exoticism that brings him close to other makers of what in France has always been defined as *meubles insolites* (fantasy furniture). Rateau's extraordinary championing of modelling and chasing skills allowed him to introduce superbly intricate animal, bird and other natural forms as decorative motifs in his pieces. A coiled snake rears up to become a lamp, birds' wings and feet frame looking-glasses, and leaf shapes are transformed so as to become the structural elements of tables or chairs. Such

manipulations of the natural world reveal a certain connection with the types of 'primitive' African or Oceanic art that were becoming much admired by Parisian connoisseurs at this date, as well as the more conventional influence of the Egyptian and Classical antiquities of which Rateau was a well-informed connoisseur.

Even among the more ostensibly conventional designers of grand furnishing pieces, many showed a remarkable degree of invention and awareness of both sculptural form and the qualities of surface decoration. Among these slightly less well-known figures I admire in particular the work of André-Léon Arbus, whose quiet mastery of softly rounded shapes often defined by precise chrome or other metal elements comes from an implicit understanding of the art of the upholsterer. In a similar way, I find the pieces conceived by André Groult inspirational for their sheer virtuosity. Exploring the use of rich and rare materials in a way so characteristic of his contemporaries and rivals, Groult revived the eighteenth-century art of covering sculptured forms with shagreen.

Shagreen – an extraordinary material, with an unmistakable hard, fine granular surface – is derived from tanning shark skin to make a form of highly decorative 'leather'. It can be successfully coloured, and a delicate celadon green has remained one of the most popular shades for shagreen since the eighteenth century. However, in the past, as a somewhat intractable material to work, shagreen was generally employed only for small objects such as knife handles, sword hilts, boxes and, in particular, *étuis* (small, ornamental cases to hold drawing instruments, travelling cutlery sets or objects for a lady's toilette). Groult's genius lay in manipulating shagreen in sections large enough to cover entire pieces of furniture, including dressing-tables, chairs

[opposite]
A fine and important desk by Jacques-Émile Ruhlmann, *c.* 1929, made in macassar ebony and gilt bronze. The 'in and out' trays set into the desktop were ahead of their time.

[left]
A four-legged centre table designed by André Groult in rosewood, the table top covered in shagreen, *c.* 1923.

[below]
The design of André-Léon Arbus's ebonized cabinet from 1933, with its crystal and gilt-bronze mounts, is utterly uncompromising.

and coffee tables. He also mastered a method in which shagreen is worked over curved surfaces in a way that pushes the process to its technical limits.

Jean-Michel Frank united the luxurious sensibility of the grand Parisian decorators with a cool perfection based on proportion espoused by the modernists. But where, for the most part at least, the modernists chose discreet or even deliberately inexpensive materials, Frank revelled in the use of rare and unusual ones, but would characteristically contrast the rich with the simple. In addition to his liking for the traditional materials of *grand luxe* (marble, bronze, alabaster and the like), he experimented with the use of plywood sheets or panels of stretched natural vellum for walls. Another of his innovations was to revive the use of decorative straw-work in the eighteenth-century manner. He also explored the possibilities of vellum as an elegant and surprisingly durable surface material for furniture, and delighted in echoing its dry, pale surface with light fittings cast in plaster of Paris by his friends Diego and Alberto Giacometti. The sculptors also used their bronze-casting skills to create tables, chairs and lanterns with irregular surfaces and a rich green patination that made their pieces resemble ancient archaeological finds.

Frank's masterful blending of unusual but harmonious materials, his liking for a bold horizontal emphasis and an overall preference for relatively spare effects give the interiors he created – such as those for his great patron Marie-Laure de Noailles – a feeling of space and repose that brings his work ultimately as close to the aesthetic of the more refined modernists as to that of the Parisian decorators. More than any other designer of the period, it is he who bridges the gap – at one time held to be absolute, though I believe incorrectly – between these two worlds.

[preceding pages]
Gosling based the design of this project in Hampstead, North London, on the SS *Normandie* ocean liner launched in 1935. The large bookcase is a bold mixture of American walnut and English sycamore, while the rosewood credenza on the right is inset with polished nickel and vellum door panels. The back walls are lit by mirrored and gilded-linen sconces.

[below and opposite]
In the same house, one wall of the dining room is hung with verre églomisé panels by Peter Gorman. Their design is based on lacquerwork by Armand-Albert Rateau (see pages 116–17). The table is solid English sycamore and highly polished santos rosewood.

[previous pages]
The coffee table in the drawing room is made in mahogany. Its vellum inset panels balance the lighting, created by Fine Art Lamps, and the hand-woven inset carpet by The Rug Company.

[left and below]
The master bedroom has pieces made in dark-stained mahogany in a distinctive 1930s style that follows the period's rules of proportion.

[opposite]
The triple-curved principal staircase was created together with Christian Garnett Architects. It sweeps down to a black lacquer table with a frieze of faceted, bevelled mirrors. The extraordinary fibre-optic chandelier was made by Sharon Marston using hundreds of pieces of hand-blown Venetian glass.

[opposite]
Detail of the rosewood sideboard in the dining room showing the deep fluting that can also be found on the pedestals of the dining table.

[right]
A close-up of a demi-lune console table, one of a pair made for the entrance hall. The carved scrolls are water-gilded in white gold and based on designs by André-Léon Arbus.

At the centre of this impressive space is an Art Deco-style rug designed by Gosling for The Rug Company collection. It was created to reflect the architecture of Hay's Wharf, built in London between 1928 and 1932. The rug's silk lines are separated by a hand-clipped 1mm gap to make them crisper. Above the fireplace hangs a contemporary bas-relief frieze by the sculptor Jonathon Coleman.

[opposite]
A tall cabinet and open display cabinet in harewood (stained sycamore) for an apartment in central London. Both are based on the architecture of the Daily Express building in Fleet Street (see page 119) and its adherence to the Art Deco rule of the three-stepped top moulding.

[below left]
The two cabinets are made in walnut and light grey harewood, with bone stringing and turned bone handles. The red-lacquer mirror and chest of drawers were designed by Gosling to contrast with the harewood pieces.

[below]
The drawers for the tall cabinet are graded in size, with the deepest at the bottom and the shallowest at the top. All have hand-dovetailed solid English oak sides with walnut and harewood fronts.

[opposite]
A pair of mahogany cabinets with inset panels of gold-leafed verre églomisé flanks the fireplace in a house in Belgravia. The interior design is by Joanna Wood.

[right]
The verre églomisé panels had three black lines painted onto the glass before the gold leaf was layered onto the reverse. The use of triple motifs in detailing was a predominant feature of Art Deco.

[preceding pages]
A library and desk made in santos rosewood with linear inlays of polished brass for a London house by Robert Adam. The interior design was created by Anna Owens.

[left]
The shape of the desk was based on a famous piece by Jacques-Émile Ruhlmann (see page 120), with its wonderful half-moon front. Its curved form is accentuated by the radiating grain of the rosewood, which continues across a lift-up section for electric cables.

[opposite]
Niches set into the panelling are designed to open up the space visually and to house artworks and sculptures without interrupting the horizontal brass lines.

[opposite and right]
There is a very subtle indent in the desk's profile to accommodate the user. Discreet pedestal locks, hidden in the sides of the desk, are used to open small doors, all of which have mitered edges to minimize their thickness.

[following pages]
A full view of Gosling's library and desk within their town house setting. Their exceptional craftsmanship is evident in the book-matching of the rosewood grain on the left-hand panels. Anna Owens chose gilded coffering for the ceiling and hand-woven silk rugs for the floor.

[opposite and right]
This occasional table for an apartment in central London was made in Bombay rosewood with brass inlays. The surface is CITES-approved crocodile skin. Three tapered legs support the frieze, and stability is improved by the addition of a circular base, also inlaid with crocodile. It was designed to echo the Anish Kapoor mirror that hangs above.

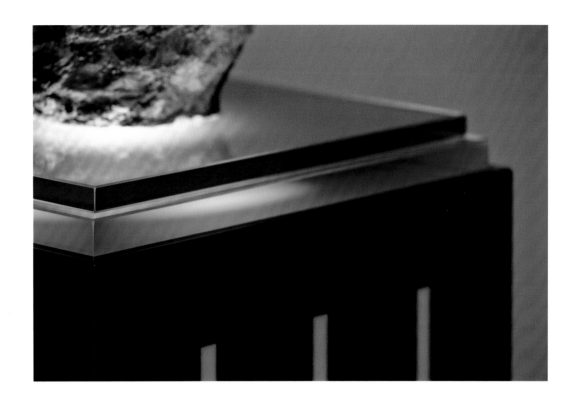

[left]
This three-stepped Deco-style plinth is made in glass, black lacquer and bone. The top is lit in order to highlight the sculpture.

[below and opposite]
The pair of mahogany stools flanking the plinth were based on a design by Jacques-Émile Ruhlmann. The base of the plinth has a shadow gap of brushed steel, whereas the stools' legs are capped in brushed brass. The interior design of this apartment in Chelsea, London, is by Chancery St James Designs.

[opposite and below]
For an apartment in Belgravia Gosling designed an extraordinary bar in harewood, English sycamore, bone stringing, and inset panels of hand-cut bronze straw by Jallu Ébénistes. The top section features individual glass-holders wrapped in leather, and the upper part has inset lighting. The upper surface is made of glass and houses lighting for sculpture. The bar contains various pull-out sections for chopping lemons – an important element of the client's brief.

[left and below]
A bar in three sections made in American walnut with inlays of slip-matched santos rosewood, polished nickel, aged leather and sapphire-jewel shagreen. It was designed to hold a silver cocktail shaker in the centre compartment, with pull-out mirrored surfaces for mixing cocktails and extendible wine racks in rosewood.

[opposite]
Aged leather was chosen to provide contrast with the star-burst rosewood design and the pull-out drinks surfaces in blue shagreen.

[opposite and right]
An Art Deco-inspired grey sycamore
media cabinet created for the master
bedroom of a house in Holland Park,
London. The three-panel mirrored
surface, which holds the television
screen, is framed by rounded edges
and fluted mouldings in the style of
an Art Deco cinema. The handles are
handmade in polished chrome with
bone inserts.

[preceding pages]
Nell Gwynn House in Sloane Avenue,
London, designed by the architect
G. K. Green, featured cutting-edge
detailing when it opened in 1936.
The bronze ceiling above the revolving
door and the door itself are original,
but much of the 1930s interior has
sadly been lost over the years.

[opposite and right]
Together with the sculptor Jonathon
Coleman, Gosling designed an Art Deco
frieze of interlocking dance figures that
now runs around the lobby of Nell
Gwynne House. There is also a pair of lit
plinths in black lacquer by Gosling in the
two entrance bays, and a series of new
chrome standard lamps and occasional
tables that re-create an impression of
Art Deco splendour.

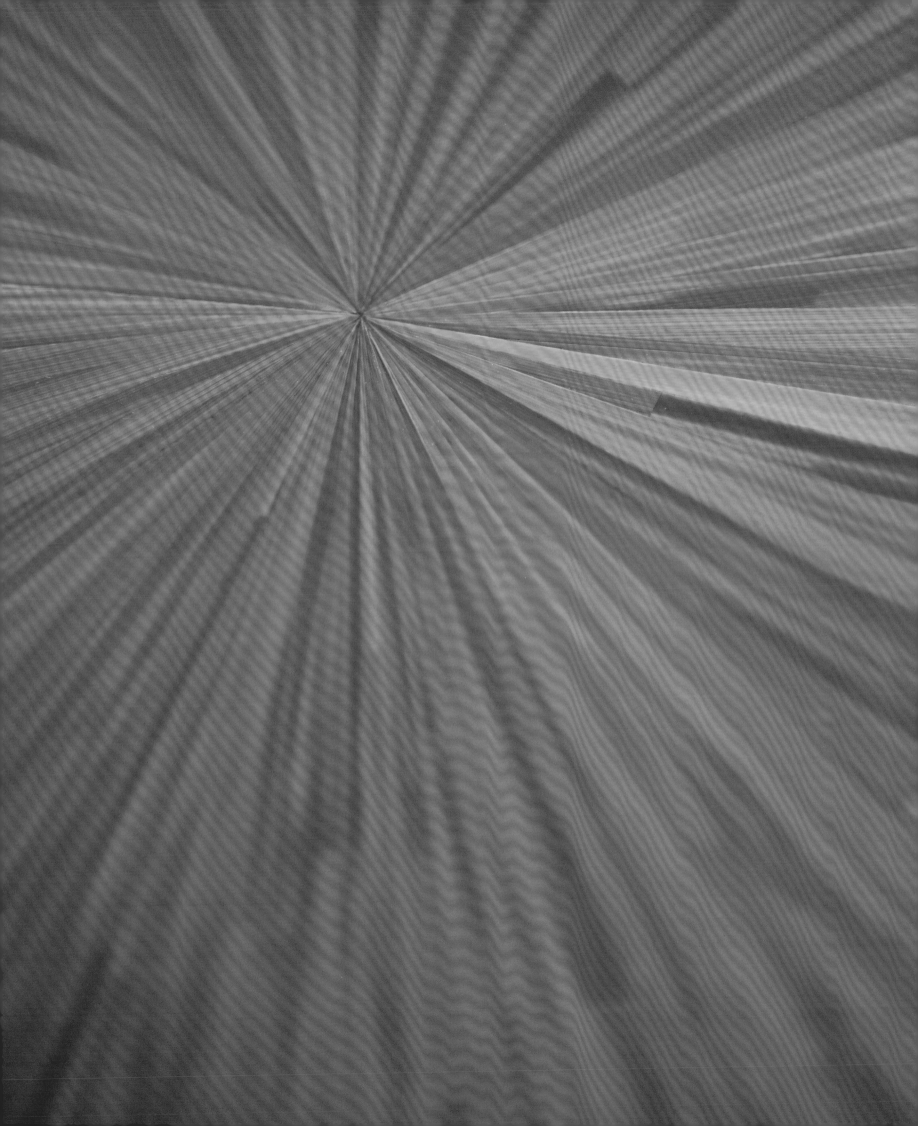

Twentieth-Century Modernism
1910–1970

THE DESIGN RULES

· Form and structure revealed ·
· Absence of ornament; the design is pared down to its essence: 'less is more' ·
· Floating planes ·
· Clean lines and fluidity of design shapes ·
· An emphasis on the horizontal ·

MATERIALS

Concrete, steel, glass, chrome
Tubular steel
Book-matched marble, onyx and alabaster veneers; travertine

Rosewood, stained black oak, natural oak, sycamore, ash, teak
Laminated woods, plywood, stretched leather
Black lacquer, Bakelite, Lucite

LEADING FIGURES

Frank Lloyd Wright
[1867–1959]
American architect, interior and furniture designer. His iconic building is the Guggenheim Museum, New York. His pioneering modern houses such as Fallingwater made striking use of horizontal, cantilevered structures.

Peter Behrens
[1868–1940]
German architect, theorist and teacher, trained first as a painter and bookbinder. A founding member of the Deutsche Werkbund, he pioneered the transition from Art Nouveau to a classical-inspired modernism. His influence was crucial in the development of Walter Gropius, Mies van der Rohe and Le Corbusier.

Eileen Gray
[1878–1976]
Architect and furniture designer. Born in Ireland, Gray initially made her name in France with decorative furniture created from lavish materials. Many of her later classic modernist chrome and leather pieces have remained in production. Her most significant architectural achievement was the stylish cliff house she built for herself in the south of France, known as E1027.

Walter Gropius
[1883–1969]
German architect, product designer, teacher; founding director of the Bauhaus. His designs ranged from the first truly modernist factory buildings to iconic door handles epitomizing the notion that 'form follows function'.

Mies van der Rohe
[1886–1969]
German architect and designer, and the third and final director of the Bauhaus. His Barcelona Pavilion of 1929 was widely influential for its use of rich materials in a modernist context. Following the closure of the Bauhaus in 1933 he went to America, where his meticulously detailed glass and steel buildings set a standard for mid-century commercial and domestic architecture.

Le Corbusier
[1887–1965]
Architect, furniture designer and a principal theorist of the International Modern Movement. Born Charles-Édouard Jeanneret in Switzerland, he changed his name and adopted French nationality. He designed both inventive single buildings, such as a chapel at Ronchamp, and high-density housing according to his own mathematical system of proportion, 'Modulor'.

Carlo Scarpa
[1906–1978]
Architect, furniture and glass designer. Living and working in Venice, Scarpa drew on the city's architectural and glass-making traditions. His work, influenced by Le Corbusier, was guided by a preoccupation with the mathematical rules of design and proportion. He was able to find ultra-modern but sympathetic design solutions to the adapting of ancient buildings.

Charles Eames
[1907–1978]
Furniture designer; in partnership with his wife, Ray Eames (1912–1988), he perfected the technique of moulding plywood to create complex, organic forms. Later the couple explored the use of cast resins and wire in the mass production of office and domestic furniture.

Eero Saarinen
[1910–1961]
Son of the celebrated Finnish architect Eliel Saarinen, he arrived in the United States with his parents in 1923. Exploring the wider possibilities of architectural form, in partnership with Charles Eames he also designed furniture. His most famous pieces are the cast resin *Tulip* and *Pedestal* chairs of 1956, manufactured by Knoll.

Harry Bertoia
[1915–1978]
Furniture designer. Born in Italy, he moved to Detroit at the age of 15. Coming under the influence of Gropius and Charles Eames, he designed inventive wire-mesh furniture pieces including the *Diamond* chair. Many of his designs were produced by Knoll in the 1950s.

Robin Day
[1915–2010]
British furniture designer and industrial and product designer. The creator of a number of classic furniture designs for mass production, Day worked closely with the manufacturers S. Hille, steering their range from mostly traditionally styled wooden pieces towards modernist forms using new materials. Their ultimate creation was a polypropylene stacking chair, the *Polyprop* (1963), that was heat-resistant, light, strong and almost indestructible.

The dawn of the twentieth century witnessed an extraordinary change in the world. Just as new discoveries and startling advances in technology came thick and fast, changing the way things had been done for centuries, so did innovation and revolution in the arts lead to a rejection of the accepted patterns of the past. Now the avant-garde embraced not only art and music, but also architecture and design, creating a restless desire for the new. The spirit of the age was suddenly more international than ever before, and almost aggressively forward-looking: the intellectual and artistic climate of Europe and the United States was increasingly one of restless expectation. Celebration of 'the modern' and an unexpected acceptance of, and delight in, all things new and challenging came to define the age.

Among the thinkers and practitioners who advanced the cause of progress, the architect and theorist Adolf Loos holds a special place. As a pupil of Otto Wagner, he began his career within the context of the old imperial capital of Vienna, where architects and patrons vied to create not only interiors of great opulence, but façades encrusted with carving, gilding and richly coloured pattern. At first tentatively eschewing the florid decorative effects of his rivals and contemporaries, Loos began to design domestic and commercial buildings in which the structural elements were more obviously expressed and from which he progressively banished ornament entirely, relying on a highly developed sense of proportion and the visual impact of carefully modulated plain surfaces.

In parallel with his active, though in fact never highly successful, architectural practice, Loos also found plenty of time to formulate and publish his ideas. In his seminal lecture of 1910, 'Ornament and Crime', he made what would become one of the most famous and fundamental statements of the Modern Movement. According to Loos, it is ornament, being by its nature subject to fashion, that makes buildings and domestic objects go out of fashion and thus become obsolete. His observation of this inexorable process led him, he claimed, to the logical conclusion that ornament is therefore 'criminally' wasteful and immoral. 'The evolution of culture,' he wrote, 'marches with the elimination of ornament from useful objects.' Beauty for Loos lay in the inherent quality of materials, unadorned and in strict adherence to functionality. Design would never be the same again.

In those times of aesthetic experimentation in the first decades of the century, minimalist and rationalist aspirations in architecture and design often went hand-in-hand with socialist ideals and progressive theories concerning social planning. In the early days of the international Modern Movement – its 'heroic' phase, as it is sometimes called – many of the leading protagonists espoused modernism as the style of 'the people'; these pioneers believed fervently that they were making a brave new world. Even if at times their attempts to reconcile the ideal of building for the many with the desire to build well using fine materials led inevitably to compromise, the modernists always insisted that they occupied the high moral ground: theirs, they claimed, was the one true style. To a somewhat surprising extent this is still the case today. As a designer who delights in working in many different styles, I do find this aspect of the modernist ethos curious.

Much has been written about the origins of modernism, and many claims have been advanced for the importance of various forerunners. Writing nearly half a century ago, and with clear memories of the movement's early days, the great design historian Nikolaus Pevsner in his *Sources of Modern Architecture and Design* (1968) argued persuasively that seeds

[opposite]
Marcel Breuer's 'Wassily' chair of 1925
– also known as the Model B3 – presented
a daring new structural form in steel
tubing.

[below]
The iconic 'Red–Blue Chair' designed by
Gerrit Rietveld in 1923.

of the modernist ethos were to be found in the ideas of the Arts and Crafts Movement in Britain and, strange as it might seem, in the wild, deliberately unhistorical inventions of Art Nouveau. Perhaps rather more obviously, Pevsner also pointed to the major influence of the robust heritage of iron industrial building, early railway architecture and the bold creations of engineers including Gustave Eiffel.

Modernism as we recognize it today emerged most powerfully in Austria and Germany in the years immediately before and following the First World War. Two key organizations set the scene. The first, the Wiener Werkstätte, led by Josef Hoffmann, pioneered the creation of furniture, metalwares and domestic objects conceived in a fresh, rectilinear style, but still recognizably the products of an old-fashioned craft system. The second, the Deutsche Werkbund, was founded in Germany by Hermann Muthesius with the aim of reconciling craftwork with more advanced ideas concerning the use of new materials and mass-production methods. Influenced by the example of both these organizations, the Bauhaus was founded in 1919 by Walter Gropius in Weimar, the small but energetic and intellectually forward-looking republic that emerged, for a while, from the ashes of the German defeat of 1918. Though conceived at first as a school for the makers of furnishings and household goods, and to train a new breed of product designers (an architecture department would come only later), the Bauhaus became the true cradle of modernism.

As a designer and teacher, Gropius promoted the ideal of art and technology as a 'new unity'. From the start he ensured that the Bauhaus agenda was always concerned not only with the practical, but also the social and political, aspects of design. He claimed – surely with some echo of William Morris's ideals

– that his great aim was the creation of a 'new guild of craftsmen without the snobbery that raises an arrogant barrier between craftsmen and artists'. An awareness of new trends in painting and the study of aesthetics both played an important part in the Bauhaus project, and it is possible to trace the influence of Cubism and the new abstraction in the school's practical design curriculum. However, it was by advocating the use of factory production practices, new systems and new materials, and by exploring the fruitful possibilities of standardization, that the Bauhaus proposed the most striking solutions to the question of how to furnish the homes of the people in the machine age.

The radical stance adopted by Gropius and his dedicated band of teachers led to an emphasis on form and structure and the innovative use of inexpensive materials for both everyday domestic objects and furniture. In this, the Bauhaus furniture-makers responded to the influence of other advanced European theorists such as the De Stijl designer Gerrit Rietveld. His famous and utterly uncompromising 'Red–Blue Chair', first designed in 1917, was made initially using plain timber in stock sizes and the simplest of carpentry joints in order to facilitate mass production. It was only in 1923, in response to the stark palette of Mondrian's abstract pictures, that Rietveld created the distinctive coloured version of his chair that is held by many to be the single most significant piece of modernist furniture.

In the same way, the chairs and other pieces produced during this period according to Bauhaus principles tended towards simple geometrical designs in which the play of sculptural form generally seems to have outweighed any real concern for comfort. Thus, both intellectually and in practical terms, in intention and effect the creations of the Bauhaus ethos could be said to represent the absolute antithesis to the

exclusive, luxury-based world of the great Parisian furniture-makers and designers of the 1920s and 1930s. But is this distinction as absolute as it might seem? Today's designers, when called upon to work in a modernist mode, find that they are the inheritors of these two powerful but very disparate traditions and draw inspiration from both.

Among the most celebrated products of the great years of the Bauhaus furniture design department – still at that date called the 'cabinetmaking workshop' – were the pieces made from tubular steel to the designs of its brilliantly innovate head, Marcel Breuer. Exploiting the strength and pliability of seamless steel tubing, the production of which had been perfected only recently by the Mannesmann brothers, Breuer conceived daring, new structural forms of a kind previously impossible to achieve in any other material. The lines of his most famous chair, the Model B3, originally made with strips of tensioned cloth stretched across the light metal frame, were said to have been inspired by the curved handlebars of the designer's bicycle. Although he was not, as is often suggested, the recipient of the very first of the B3 chairs, the painter Kandinsky, who also taught at the school, did own one of the earliest examples, and for this reason the iconic design was immortalized as the 'Wassily' chair when it was later put into wider production. Later editions of the chair are instantly recognizable by the fact that the cloth back and seat of the original are replaced with rather more chic and durable black leather.

In spite of its crusading zeal, the Bauhaus – rather like the wider Modernist Movement – was never entirely free from internal rivalry and faction. When the school relocated in 1925 to Dessau, it came under a new hard-line leftist leader, Hannes Meyer, who dismissed Breuer. Meyer was himself replaced by the architect Mies van der Rohe, who effectively ran the school

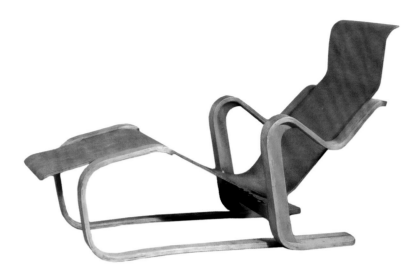

Marcel Breuer's 'Long Chair', produced for Isokon in 1935–36 in laminated plywood.

at his own expense during the short final phase of its existence in Berlin. The rising National Socialist Party was growing increasingly hostile to the Bauhaus's political stance, and in 1933, under pressure from the Gestapo, Mies and his staff closed the school. The paradoxical effect of this forced winding-up of the Bauhaus project was the creation of a diaspora of inventive talent and creativity, as the school's best thinkers and designers fled Germany and carried the modernist message to the United Kingdom and America.

In England, Breuer continued his experiments with new materials. Working with the innovative firm Isokon, he now explored the use of laminated plywood, then an entirely novel idea, which allowed the manufacture of subtle shapes that could be curved in more than one plane. Built up from multiple thin layers of wood, with the grain laid in opposing directions, plywood possessed great strength combined with a certain flexibility. Exploiting these qualities to the full, Breuer created plywood masterpieces every bit as daring as his tubular-metal chairs. The most famous of these Isokon pieces is his 'Long Chair' of 1935–36, a self-indulgent lounger in which the richly sinuous, cantilevered form seems deliberately counterpointed by the pale simplicity of the inexpensive material. To me, the Long Chair, with its contrasting plain surfaces and visibly layered edges that reveal and express the constructional method, is one of the most exhilarating statements of modernity in furniture design.

While furniture design enjoyed a period of extraordinary inventiveness during the early, exploratory phase of the Modern Movement – and almost every architect and furniture-maker seems to have felt the need to create at least one iconic chair – the true essence of modernity lay in its ethos of the integrity of architecture, interior and furnishings. The idea of the

Gesamtkunstwerk, or 'total work of art', is generally held to have been formulated by Richard Wagner to express his search for an all-embracing experience to which the elements of music, theatre, stage design and lighting all contributed. The concept was enthusiastically taken up and expanded by modernist architects such as Gropius to suggest an ideal in which every aspect of architecture and design united to inspire and shape an entire form of existence or – as we would now call it – lifestyle.

Among the founding-fathers of this approach was the Swiss-born architect Charles-Édouard Jeanneret, who adopted France as his home and the memorably simplified pseudonym Le Corbusier as his name. Le Corbusier had early fallen under the influence of Gropius and Mies, but took their ideas even farther in his search for a pure essence of design and theory of life for the modern century. In his major treatise of 1923, *Vers une architecture*, he suggested that 'the styles are a lie', and went on to make the most famous pronouncement of the Modern Movement: 'The house is a machine for living in.'

Le Corbusier's early studies included a two-month period measuring and reflecting upon the Parthenon. From this intensive scrutiny he began to develop the theories of proportion in buildings and its relation to the scale of the human form that he would elaborate as his 'Modulor' system. Le Corbusier's Modulor proposed a unit of measurement based upon the height of a man's raised arm. Intended to reconcile the mismatch between Anglo-Saxon feet and inches (the imperial system) and the continental metre (the metric system), the Modulor inevitably recalled Leonardo da Vinci's much earlier formulation based on his image of the ideal 'Vitruvian Man'.

Subsequently, Le Corbusier also adopted the concept of the golden section, the arcane concept known in the ancient world for creating perfect proportion. The golden section

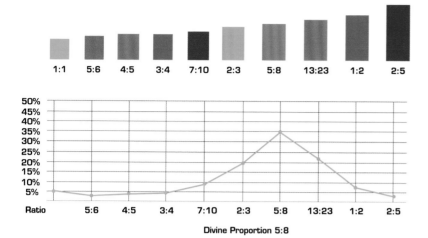

1:1 5:6 4:5 3:4 7:10 2:3 5:8 13:23 1:2 2:5

50%
45%
40%
35%
30%
25%
20%
15%
10%
5%

Ratio 5:6 4:5 3:4 7:10 2:3 5:8 13:23 1:2 2:5

Divine Proportion 5:8

[left]
This experiment was devised by Gustav Fechner in the late 1800s to ascertain which proportions of a rectangular shape were most pleasing to the eye. Most people viewed a 5:8 ratio as the optimum choice.

[below]
Le Corbusier's modular scale of proportions, influenced by Vitruvian Man. It was first used comprehensively in the planning of the Unité d'Habitation in Marseilles, 1945–52. Illustration from *Science et Vie*, October 1955.

dictates that, where a line is divided into two unequal parts, the proportion of the shorter to the longer should be identical to that of the longer in relation to the whole. In practice, this can be calculated as a ratio of about 1:1.62. From this ratio it is also possible to create rectangular shapes of which the dimensions and areas possess the same 'divine' proportion and thus appear aesthetically pleasing. In a world in which 'the styles' derided by Le Corbusier and Loos's 'immoral' ornament have been all but banished, pleasing proportion becomes ever more important. As designers today, we can still make good use of these 'divine' ratios in order to create a sense of harmony and the subtly satisfying feeling of repose in a design project.

Opinion is divided on which aspects of the work produced by the great modernists such as Le Corbusier and Mies van der Rohe are the most important. For some, it is Le Corbusier's ambitious housing developments that set the pattern for so much of what was to come. His Unité d'Habitation (or Cité Radieuse) in Marseille – the first of several very similar, large concrete blocks of flats – was completed in 1952. Hailed at the time as a model that would provide high-density housing for the future, the Unité possessed skilfully modulated proportions, careful detailing and bold use of colour. Sadly, these qualities were seldom matched in the huge number of dismal developments erected in cities throughout the world in the following decades; they copied Le Corbusier's basic ideas but failed to grasp the spirit and essential humanity of the original.

In some ways the other side of the modernist coin, the creation of the exquisitely crafted one-off project, is represented by two extraordinary buildings by Mies van der Rohe dating from the movement's 'heroic' age. These are his Barcelona Pavilion, erected for the German section of the International Exposition of 1929, and the Tugendhat House of the following

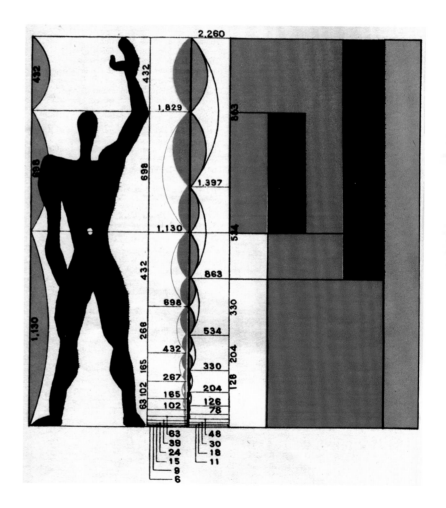

Mies van der Rohe's Pavilion for the
Barcelona World Exposition of 1929. In
1986 it was reconstructed on the
original site. The bookmatched slabs of
marble recall the rich decoration of
palace interiors, while the cut floor tiles
create their own mathematical grid.

year, built for discerning private clients in Brno in the present-day Czech Republic. Architecturally, these are both remarkable and daring structures; in terms of their interiors and furnishings they are no less exciting and have exerted a huge influence on design for more than half a century.

Mies favoured the use of modern and even novel materials, including steel and chrome contrasting with large expanses of glass, to create a feeling of unrestricted space. But he also liked to introduce traditional and luxurious materials, such as classic Roman travertine flooring and – something of a trademark detail, seen in both the Barcelona Pavilion and the Tugendhat House – richly veined onyx, alabaster or marble applied to wall surfaces using the old technique of 'book-matching' (cutting and reversing veneers to form symmetrical patterns). He thus created surfaces that, for all their sleek modern lines, also suggest the grandeur of a cathedral or of palace interiors. Mies coined two famous phrases that epitomize his search for strict simplicity and perfection: 'less is more,' he claimed, but 'God is in the details.'

In the Tugendhat House, Mies also employed exotic woods, such as the macassar ebony used to great effect as panelling in the library. Viktor Průša, who supervised the building of the villa, recalled 'the adventurous search for ebony logs with uniform veneer in import warehouses throughout Europe', and 'the cutting in the veneer factory in southern Moravia for the demanding architect'. Having a fondness for high-quality veneers for my own projects, and knowing how exacting such work is, I warm to Mies and his team.

For the 1929 Pavilion Mies also designed his totemic Barcelona chair and stool. These pieces, which figured prominently in the furnishing of the Tugendhat House as well, seem to float on razor-sharp curved supports of springy steel,

but they too, like his onyx walls, have about them a sly and knowing suggestion of opulence in the use of button-back upholstery. These classics have hardly ever been out of production since the day they were designed. As has been suggested, the design of the modern chair has become a touchstone of inventiveness. All the key architects and designers from Eileen Gray through to more recent practitioners such as Robin Day have sought to shape an iconic form. Among the mid-century moderns, Charles and Ray Eames, after several years developing their ideas, succeeded in creating their lounge chair and ottoman. Formed from moulded plywood, the Eames lounge chair was always conceived as a production line; in this, it epitomizes the aspiration of the Modern Movement to create timeless sculptural form through the use of contemporary materials and methods.

It may be claimed – especially by hard-line modernists – that the very longevity of modernism as a movement was a vindication of its original claims to be the timeless architecture and design of the people. But there is no doubt that, by a certain point in the 1970s, the tide had begun to turn quite strongly against modernism, and in particular against its most uncompromising ideals as expressed in the work of the architects who called themselves Brutalists. In truth, and for all its claims to the contrary, modernism at its best had only ever been a style for the few. While always rejecting the charge of elitism, it had never been truly popular with those for whom it claimed to exist: the people. A new generation who had grown up with a belief in a plurality of possibilities in lifestyle and who liked to juggle with styles and 'isms' would formulate new theories of design, abandoning the limiting ideas of Loos and Le Corbusier and embracing a vibrant new age of postmodernism.

[below and opposite]
A pair of cantilevered bedside tables, one of which serves as a writing desk. They are made of black lacquer with stringing of polished chrome and surfaces of black shaved shagreen. The room's interior design, by Racheline Nahon, was for a client in Highgate, London.

[opposite and below]
A console table and credenza made in solid Bombay rosewood with vellum-wrapped tops and panels. The interior design of this apartment in Chelsea, London, is by Joanna Wood.

[left]
This low table is based on Mies van der Rohe's architectural principle of 'floating planes' and on Gustav Fechner's illustration of 'perfect' proportions (see page 171).

[pages 178–79]
The panoramic view of the Grand Canal, Venice, offered by the north-facing window seat of a palazzo apartment. The building itself was painted by Claude Monet in 1908 and captures the light, colour and reflections for which the city is famous. The architecture is by Alberto Torsello and Barbara De Stefano.

[preceding pages]
The north window frames the bell tower of Santo Stefano – a view supported visually by a pair of serpentine sofas on either side and a table by Dongia in the centre. The original sofa was created in around 1950 by Vladimir Kagan; a second was made for the palazzo by Lawson Wood and upholstered in fabric by Rubelli.

[below]
A photograph by Wolfgang Tillmans sets the tonal balance for the interior. An expanding circular table with stringing in bone, made by Gosling, is accompanied by dining chairs upholstered in a green cut silk by Rubelli.

[opposite]
The library-cum-study is dominated by an exceptional elongated window that looks directly down the Grand Canal towards the Accademia Bridge. The roof space is complicated, so the library uprights are capped with Soane-style square finials at differing heights. The base is raised off the floor to create a sense of breathing space. On the right of the second illustration is a video installation by Michael Craig-Martin, whose colours are designed to fade in and out in a complex set of patterns that repeat only once every two thousand years.

[opposite and right]
A drinks cabinet in ripple sycamore and bronze inlaid created for the main living space of the Venetian apartment. The work of the sculptor Jonathon Coleman, the two bronze panels are finished in 24-carat rose gold. The top of the cabinet is gently scalloped and has shadow gaps of inset bronze.

[preceding pages and left]
A wall-mounted and cantilevered sycamore credenza for a master bedroom in Chelsea, London. This piece is inset with hand-wrapped vellum panels and features lift-up recesses for watches and cufflinks.

[below]
Behind the head of the bed are three panels upholstered in white Alicante faux suede, flanked by two mirrors and lights by Contardi. The bedspread was made by Gosling using specially woven silk from the tailor Richard James in Savile Row. It was inspired by his archive of tie designs.

[opposite]
The floating bedside tables have inset vellum tops and hand-dovetailed drawers faced in vellum.

(opposite and below)
Black lacquer cabinets for the dining room
of a nineteenth-century London house.
They are designed to hold the canteen
of silverware and crystal tableware.
The cabinet doors are hand-carved with
a series of vertical chamfered pieces.
The drawers are all lined in silk velvet.

[preceding pages]
A view of the dining room of the same London house, looking towards the entrance hall designed by Gosling with Todhunter Earle. The room is wrapped in a deep aubergine silk cut velvet. The bronze chandelier is by Hervé Van der Straeten. Designed by Gosling, the dining table is made in black lacquer with bronze stringing and edges; the table top is skived black vellum.

[below and opposite]
The pair of floating console tables either side of the solid marble fireplace are made in aubergine lacquerwork inset with bronze. The room's cornice is hand-wrapped in the same silk velvet as the walls.

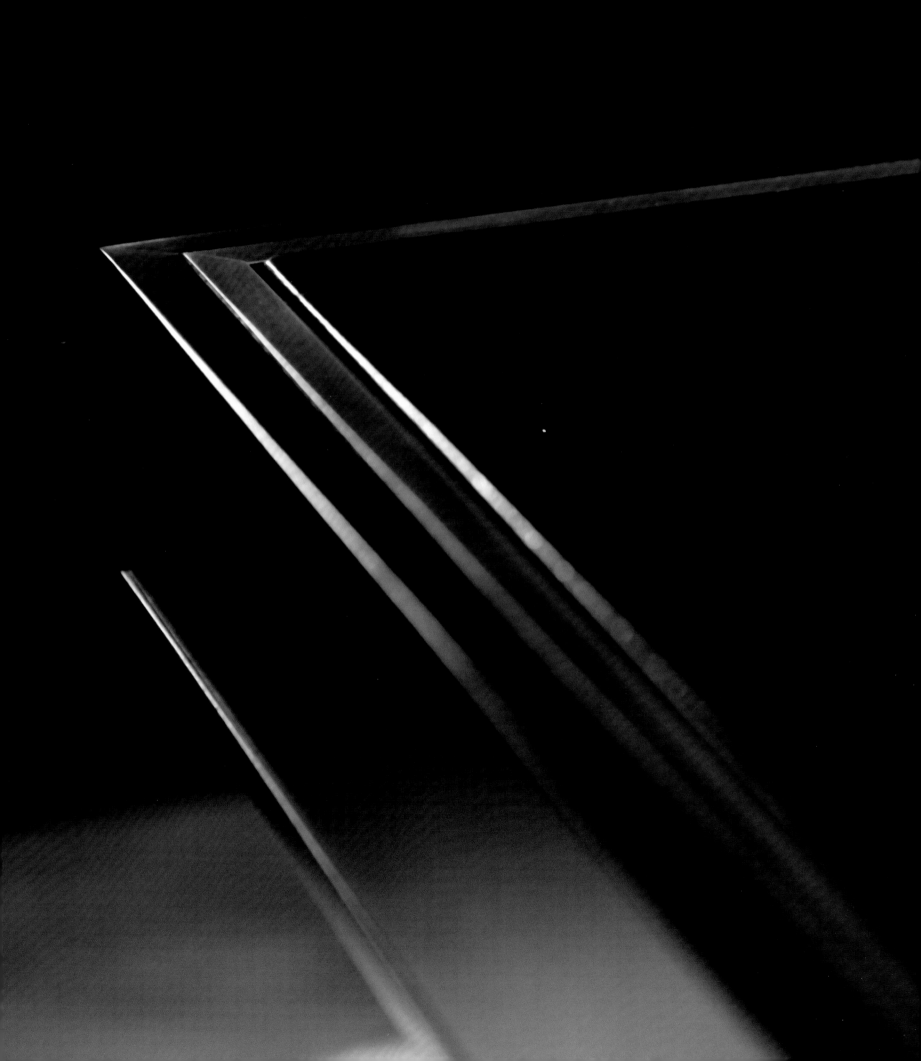

[opposite and right]
A black lacquer and rosewood dining table with inlays of white shagreen in the frieze and angular sleigh legs. The chairs are also made by hand in black lacquer. The soft furnishings and interior design are by Todhunter Earle.

[below right]
Another black lacquer dining table, this time topped with black vellum. The pedestal bases are made from glass rods that are lit internally, causing them to illuminate the glass square panels in the table top. This project in Mayfair was interior designed by Kelly Hoppen.

[preceding pages and opposite]
A black lacquer credenza with inset panels of white vellum framed with sycamore decorates a hallway for a house in Geneva. The black lacquer is hand-cracked into regularly space ridges and edged in dark bronze.

[left]
An octagonal black lacquer games table with mirrored base designed by Gosling for a house in Geneva. The interior design is by Todhunter Earle. The arms of the carver chairs, also in black lacquer, are designed with a scoop so that they can be pulled up closely to the table.

[opposite and right]
A large sycamore and bronze media cabinet in an interior designed by Joanna Wood for a house in Knights-bridge, London. The cabinet design echoes the bronze detailing found on the entrance hall doors.

[right and opposite]
The dining room interior designed
by Joanna Wood for a house in
Knightsbridge, London. Four rosewood
plinths are sliced through with acrylic to
give the illusion that the objects on top are
floating. The walls are decorated with
raised plasterwork. Made by Gosling in
Bombay rosewood, the dining table has
bone stringing inlaid around the
cross-banded frieze.

[below]
This desk for a house in Knightsbridge is
made in walnut, with ivory-coloured leather
panels and raised nickel beading.

[opposite]
The entrance hall table for a house in Knightsbridge is made in black lacquer with bone stringing and slip-matched Bombay rosewood. Beneath the table top, the frieze is made from hand-bevelled, mirrored crystal. The black lacquer and chrome base rests on a bespoke rug.

[right]
Detail of one of the dining room plinths showing the intersection of acrylic and rosewood.

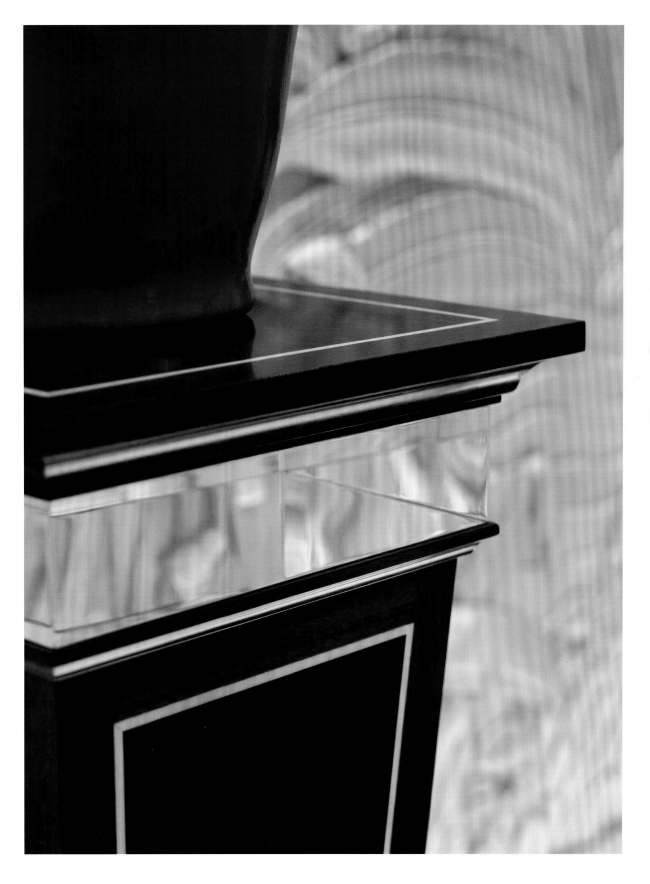

Design in the Twenty-First Century and Beyond

THE DESIGN RULES

· Fluid, asymmetric forms, and an avoidance of straight lines and rectangular shapes ·
· Experimental new materials ·
· Environmentally sustainable materials ·
· Eco-friendly technologies for lighting and heating ·
· Willingness to break all the rules ·

MATERIALS

Carbon fibre
Resins
Light blocking structural material

3D printing
DNA design data storage and transmission

LEADING FIGURES

Cesar Pelli
[b. 1926]

Argentinian-born American architect. Creator of some of the world's tallest iconic buildings, including the Petronas Twin Towers, Kuala Lumpur (1998) and One Canada Square, London (1987–1991).

Richard Rogers
[b. 1926]

Italian-born English architect. Originally in partnership with Norman Foster, Rogers became a pioneer of 'high-tech' architecture. He designed the ground-breaking exoskeleton structure of the Centre Pompidou, Paris (1977) with Renzo Piano. Later works include the Lloyd's Building, London (1978–84) and Heathrow Terminal 5 (2008).

Frank Gehry
[b. 1929]

Los Angeles-based architect, the master of the deconstructivist or post-structuralist style. His own residence at Santa Monica (1977), the titanium-clad Guggenheim Museum in Bilbao (1997) and the Walt Disney Concert Hall (2003) are his major iconic works. His furniture designs include the 'Easy Edges' collection of sculptural cardboard pieces.

Richard Meier
[b. 1934]

Neo-Corbusian architect; he uses enamelled panels and glass that share linear and spatial relationships with ramps and handrails. His design approach is generally boxy, and structures are usually white.

Norman Foster
[b. 1935]

English-born architect with a large international practice. His firm's major buildings include the Millennium Bridge, London (2000); 30 St Mary Axe, London (2004); and the Sage Gateshead arts centre (2004).

Philippe Starck
[b. 1949]

French furniture and product designer who injects notes of humour; his three-legged café chair was designed to have 'one fewer leg for waiters to fall over'.

Zaha Hadid
[b. 1950]

Born in Iraq, she has become one of the world's most creative architects and furniture designers. Her buildings include the London Aquatics Centre (2012) and the Serpentine Sackler Gallery, London (2013).

Tom Dixon
[b. 1959]

Protagonist of the 'creative salvage' movement of the 1980s, he went on to design products for Habitat. He is a champion of innovative materials and techniques.

We live in the most exciting times of technological innovation. In terms of the extraordinary new possibilities that are opened up to designers by the emergence of new materials and the rapid development of novel methods of manufacture, the future looks almost limitless – or, if you prefer, might appear scarily unchartable. For this reason, the idea of constantly measuring ourselves and what we do against the achievements of the past seems to me to be a key part of progress. The need on the one hand to preserve traditional craft skills and to do all that we can to secure the sustainability of our tried and tested materials, and on the other to grasp the potential inherent in new techniques and materials, should surely never be incompatible. Together they offer the most extraordinary possibilities for the creation of work that is innovative but informed by the best that has been done in the past – work that can measure itself proudly in relation to all that has gone before.

In historical terms we stand on a cusp. Certainly, many of the techniques and materials of furniture-making that we employ remain, even today, surprisingly unchanged since ancient times. Kipling's amusing poem of 1922, 'A Truthful Song', tells of 'Pharaoh the Great' and Noah visiting modern bricklayers on a building site, and a boat-builders' yard. Recognizing almost all their tools and materials, they chorus: 'How very little, since things was made, / Anything alters in any one's trade!' This is perhaps most true of the high-quality craftsmanship and expensive materials that we associate with top-end, luxury-market goods. But since Kipling's heyday we have grown up with the twentieth-century's headlong rush towards innovation in techniques and the crucial idea of mass-production as part of our thinking. Marcel Breuer's tubular-steel cantilever chairs and laminated plywood furniture have

been with us since the 1930s, and the famous injection-moulded polypropylene stacking chair designed by Robin Day since 1962; for designers of my generation it is hard to imagine a school assembly hall or public building without at least a few of these serviceable and essentially democratic classics. But today the old distinctions fall away, and the correlations between handicraft and expense, and mass manufacture and economy, are being entirely recalibrated.

Certainly there will always be a call for the finest workmanship – the application of vellum or shagreen to a complex sculptural form, for example, that can be achieved only by the combination of a practised eye and the most skilled hand. Today, however, the most perfect and exquisite marquetry is created by a laser cutter following a computerized pattern with the utmost precision. Similarly, the most intricate of filigree designs can be created on metals by the seeming magic – and at almost inconceivable speed – of photo-etching technology. Guided by computer programming, this process replaces at a stroke hours of intensive hand work and actually differs little from the now worldwide standard means of creating printed circuitry in the electronics industry. Already we live in an era in which the design, furnishing and decoration of an oligarch's floating palace of a yacht have as much in common with the installation of a Space Shuttle's instrument control panel as with the traditional skills of the boatyard.

Another development of huge potential in the creation of furniture and other luxury goods – and one in which I have a great interest – is the use of carbon fibre. This exciting new material was first discovered and exploited in the 1960s and 1970s. Its unique property is its extraordinary strength-to-weight ratio, and the more the content of carbon can be increased in any structure, the more strength it delivers. It was

[opposite]
Designed by Tom Dixon in 1987,
the 'S' chair is finished with rush woven
by the basket-making industry.

[below]
The hugely successful polycarbonate
'Louis Ghost' chair, designed by Philippe
Starck in 2002. Since its launch over
1.5 million have been sold.

first adopted by military designers for use in combat aviation but, as carbon fibre's potential became more widely appreciated, it was quickly embraced by designers working in the motor-racing industry and in other so-called 'super-manufacturing' contexts. Over the last decades carbon fibre has become increasingly interesting and accessible to furniture designers, for whom the material's lightweight strength and highly durable nature lend themselves to entirely new types of pieces.

One application in particular that has caused a sea change in current practice is the making of deck furniture for luxury boats that is resilient to corrosion by the elements. Whereas previously chairs and other items of outside equipment were cumbersome, required almost constant repainting to preserve a smart appearance and were often thrown away after no more than five seasons' use, now carbon-fibre pieces, although necessarily produced with a considerable initial cost, are light and elegant, and, when finished with high-specification painted finishes originally developed for aircraft, remain maintenance-free and seem virtually indestructible.

In almost all areas of manufacturing, the last thirty years have witnessed the introduction of first mechanized and then computer-controlled production methods. A further refinement of this inexorable process of pushing boundaries would, until recently, have been deemed to belong to the realm of science fiction rather than the factory floor. Today, three-dimensional printing technology has become a reality. Already a working handgun has been successfully 'printed', and the possibilities appear endless for the further, and one might hope more benign, development of such techniques – both at the scale of nano-technology and in the creation of a wide range of useful commodities, including furniture. At a macro scale, an admittedly cruder, but also potentially fruitful, method of

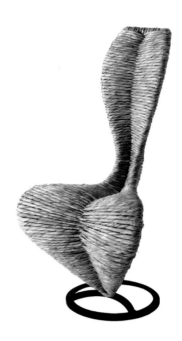

employing extruded rubber or plastic to create bold and bright domestic objects has been pioneered by the endlessly innovative left-field designer Tom Dixon.

Design and manufacture are also affected by the extraordinary size of world markets. In part, demand is clearly stimulated simply by the unprecedented availability of, and access to, information that has resulted from the internet revolution. Anyone can now discover the entire history of the development of furniture from a million available images, and in the same way everyone can keep abreast of the latest fashions; we can instantly find – and just as instantly click to buy – things in any style from anywhere in the world. A fascinating illustration of this trend is the phenomenal success of the 'Louis Ghost' chair. Designed by the unpredictable genius of contemporary French furniture, Philippe Starck, in 2002, this now ubiquitous piece was based on a Louis XVI *fauteuil*, but the historic form was re-imagined and transformed in its effect by being re-created in transparent injection-moulded polycarbonate. The resulting piece has a stylistic ambiguity and a shifting presence; consequently, it is at home, it seems, in almost any architectural or stylistic context, from a period panelled room to the most adventurous modern interior. Astoundingly, Starck has to date sold over 1.5 million 'Louis Ghost' chairs, while a further unknowable number of copies and fakes have also entered into circulation worldwide.

As in past centuries, some of the most striking recent furniture designs have been created by architects. In the same way that figures including William Kent and Robert Adam in the eighteenth, Augustus Pugin in the nineteenth and Mies van der Rohe in the twentieth centuries all found furniture design to be an activity that complemented, and indeed stretched, their imaginations as architects, so too have a number of leading

practitioners today explored aesthetic possibilities and even enriched the architectural vocabulary of their major projects through working at times on a more intimate, domestic scale. Zaha Hadid, for example, renowned for the volumetric sweep of her vast roof structures – her celebrated London Aquatics Centre for the 2012 Olympics is one example – has brought her determination to turn her back on traditional orthogonal structures in favour of audacious asymmetry to her designs for furniture. This pursuit of experimental form and fluid structure is seen at its best in such pieces as her 'Mesa' table, which has been aptly described as 'a microcosmic extrusion of the spatial ideas inherent in [her] architecture'. 'Form doesn't follow only function,' says the architect herself, 'but instead is drawn along by the narrative of the plan and flow of space.'

In fact, if any single unifying factor is to be discerned in the architectural trends of the last few decades and looks likely to inform further experimentation in the coming years, it is this desire to escape from the visual limitations and structural dictates of the square, the rectangular, the perpendicular, the horizontal and, above all, the spatially predictable. Architects and designers as diverse in their ideals and practice as Frank Gehry (Guggenheim Museum, Bilbao), Renzo Piano (The Shard, London), Daniel Libeskind (Jewish Museum, Berlin, and the unbuilt extension to the Victoria and Albert Museum, London, known as 'the Spiral') and Norman Foster (30 St Mary Axe, London) each in their own way exemplifies this worldwide trend, which can be traced back to the daring outlines of 1960s projects, such as Jørn Utzon's Sydney Opera House, and even beyond, to Le Corbusier's ground-breaking concrete chapel at Ronchamp.

Architectural projects on this scale of ambition need to be underpinned by structural engineering of the highest order. As

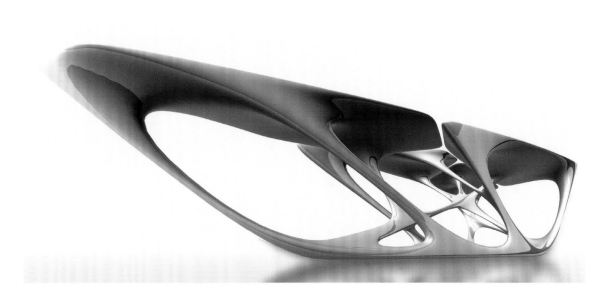

buildings become more experimental and free-form, the complexity of that engineering, and the amount of data involved, multiply at an astounding rate. Even the creation of a small but complex piece of furniture may now entail a great deal of computer modelling. Of course, the creation of subtle shapes rather than merely straight lines in architecture is nothing new. The so-called *entasis*, that almost imperceptible curve that swells the profile of the columns of a Greek temple towards their base, to create a sense of perfection and 'correct' the visual anomaly by which long horizontal baselines appear to sag at their centre, was conceived by the ancients and has been understood and applied for millennia. *Entasis* can be calculated mathematically, but it is generally held that many of the great builders worked intuitively, guided by what was essentially a notional rule. The creation of buildings today is technically so demanding and the tolerances so fine that the amount of information required constantly threatens to spiral out of control. As in so many aspects of modern life, the creation, processing and storage of this rising tide of data seems to be one of the crucial problems we face.

Curiously, however, this question of the management of data in design processes brings me right back to my starting point in the introduction to this book, where I spoke of the fascination and personal significance that DNA holds for me. As a result of recent work carried out at the European Bioinformatics Institute, Cambridge, by Nick Goldman and Ewan Birney, it appears that in addition to holding the key to the very building blocks of life, the double helix could also play an extraordinary future role as a kind of vast data storage system for unimaginably large amounts of information. Using the chemical 'letters' that make up a strand of DNA – G, A, T and C – to encode the 1s and 0s of large samples of

sound, pictures and text expressed in binary form, they emailed their new sequence to a bio-tech company in California, which then transformed it into physical DNA material. Sent back to Cambridge in freeze-dried powder form, the sample resembled nothing more than a speck of dust. But by using a DNA coding machine, the Cambridge team discovered that they were able to 'read' the sample and to recover the original data with 100 per cent accuracy. The information contained in the experimental sequence included Shakespeare's complete sonnets, film of Martin Luther King's 'I had a dream' speech and, to my delight, the famous paper from *Nature* (1952) in which Crick, Watson, Franklin and my father announced their discovery of the double-helix structure of DNA. The Cambridge team believe that a single cup of DNA material could store the equivalent of 100,000 hours of high-definition film.

The capacity to store information on this scale, and without the use of energy, suggests the most extraordinary possibilities, not least in areas of human creativity such as architecture and design. I like to think that our powers of invention will be stimulated by such prospects, and that there are effectively no limits to what we can hope to achieve. But even if, in a not too distant future, much of our everyday furniture could be supplied on a global print-on-demand basis or grown through genetic modification, I also fervently believe that there will always be a place in our culture for the finest creations of hand and eye. It is a measure of great civilizations that they continually embrace the best of the new, but that they also remember to value and learn from the best of the old.

Gosling worked in conjunction with New Land Solutions and Ian Adam-Smith to design a family room that converts into a cinema in a Queen Anne house in London. Once the low table has receeded the sofa moves forward, the cinema seating rises up and the transformation of the room is complete. The Deco-style rug design was based on the BBC logo of the 1930s and made by The Rug Company.

[preceding pages]

The wine vaults of the Queen Anne house are bespoke, designed by Gosling to be encased in sleek harewood and polished chrome wall panelling.

[opposite]

The elevator, seen on the far left of the image, is designed in black lacquer punctured with thousands of back-lit drill holes. Viewed together, they depict St James's Park and the Victoria Memorial in London, thus turning the elevator into a kind of illuminated light box.

[below]

The curved harewood panelling guides you to a powder room lined in verre églomisé and on to the family room-cum-cinema.

[left and opposite]
A black lacquer occasional table made in turned and ribbed sections of sycamore for the Gosling for Todhunter Collection. It was designed to contrast with the classical oak panelling of the interior of a house in Geneva.

Classic
Craftsmanship

[page 224]
A craftsman adds the final touches to a pair of black lacquer half-moon cabinets. The hand-gilded design is cross-hatched in a process known as 'penning'; while it resembles scrimshaw work, here it is lacquer, not bone or ivory, that is engraved. Penwork creates an illusion of shadow on the gilded motifs.

[left]
The same pair of black lacquer half-moon cabinets at the DKT workshop. Successive layers of lacquerwork are required to give the right depth of finish.

[below and opposite]
The extraordinary hand-carving of Christine Palmer, from Carvers and Gilders, was part of a complex process to produce a Chippendale-style chinoiserie overmantel mirror designed by Gosling for a dining room in Eaton Square, London. A full-sized working drawing can be seen on the wall behind Palmer. By referring to fragments of Chippendale gilding, we were able to create and tonally balance the mirror using the same processes as Thomas Chippendale in the eighteenth century.

I find that researching, learning and understanding the boundless possibilities presented by materials are, for me, endlessly exciting. From discovering finishes in a museum and working out how to achieve them, to discussing new materials such as carbon fibre as they start to become available to the wider British crafts industry, all these experiences inform my role in designing contemporary furniture for today. In the same way I am always aware of the centuries of thought processes and skilled craftsmanship that have enabled us to reinvent the designs of the past within the constraints and discipline of traditional craftsmanship. This knowledge allows me to create contemporary pieces of furniture and interiors while respecting the evolution of tradition.

To give one example, I recently made a pair of black lacquer commodes whose half-moon doors are decorated with a gilded design. This used a modern adaptation of a technique known as 'scrimshaw', in which a design is engraved by hand onto whalebone or ivory and then filled with ink. Here, the design was engraved into the gilded surface of gold leaf through a technique known as 'penning', which created the illusion of shadow by revealing the black lacquer underneath.

Even among the exceptionally skilled craftsmen that I work with, finding the exact terminology of the techniques we are trying to achieve is complicated. So many of the terms that we might use in our discussions have disappeared from everyday use, as well as, in some cases, a direct understanding of how to achieve a desired look.

The vellum-work on the top of 'Apse', the miniature library I created for Neale Albert, was a technique I came across at the Victoria and Albert Museum, London, in their exhibition 'Aestheticism: The Cult of Beauty' (2011). The raised gesso-work I spotted on a vellum document,

[opposite and left]
Detail of chinoiserie-style silk embroidery created by Fromental for a set of eight chairs made by Reed and Rackstraw for Gosling. The detailing and colours are exceptional. In essence, the craft of upholstery has not changed for hundreds of years.

[below]
With its fluid form, this carved shagreen-covered console table required exacting techniques to make it a reality.

water-gilded and burnished, completely stopped me in my tracks. The difficulty of finding various craftsmen to re-create this style of decoration was enormous, since it required techniques not used for over a hundred years and the close collaboration of the vellum-wrappers, master craftsmen and master gilders just for one miniature section.

The overmantel mirror designed by Gosling and carved by Christine Palmer was burnished and balanced for the dining room in Eaton Square for which it was designed – a process that took into account how much light would hit the mirror and from which direction. This was a traditional gilders' technique employed in the seventeenth and eighteenth centuries that has sadly fallen out of fashion today.

When we consider modern materials, on the other hand, we are presented with an entirely different scenario. Carbon fibre in particular offers both designers and craftsmen a great deal of potential. The inherent strength of the material allows us to create shapes and forms that would not otherwise be achievable: the sinuous curve on a pair of tub chairs, for example, has a fluidity that is only possible because of carbon fibre's strength and flexibility.

Whatever the techniques being used or considered, I am always mindful of the fact that in order to create an extraordinary piece of furniture you need access to exceptional craftsmen and craftsmanship. I owe a huge debt to the workshops and individuals all over the United Kingdom who have been involved in the creation of these exquisite pieces.

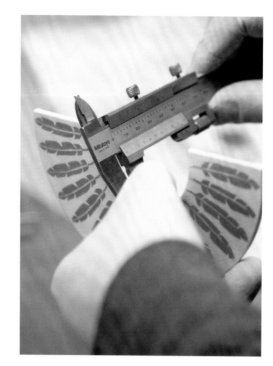

[above and opposite]
This miniature library, called 'Apse', was made for Neale Albert and based on a pavilion in Kensington Palace Gardens. Constructed in walnut, it has inlays of ebony and raised gilded vellum, with bronze medallions on the sides. It holds a miniature set of Shakespeare's plays published in 1803.

[left]
A miniature Globe Theatre, just 15 cm (6 in.) tall, also commissioned by Neale Albert. Tim Gosling drew the designs for the inside walls, which were then laser-etched into English sycamore. The leatherwork on the stage is by George Kirkpatrick. A rare and interesting star sapphire occupies centre stage, held in place by a small pedestal designed by the jeweller Vicky Ambery-Smith.

[left]
A low table made in pure carbon fibre, designed by Ruby Mogford for the Gosling Marine Collection. The top, in oiled teak, has an inset band of polished marine-grade steel.

[below and opposite]
This folding chair, designed by Phil Sturdy, has articulated joints of marine-grade steel and arms of curved teak laminate. The seating is a carbon-fibre weave that, once moulded and baked under high pressure, becomes incredibly strong. It was then sprayed white except for an open pinstripe that leaves the carbon weave visible.

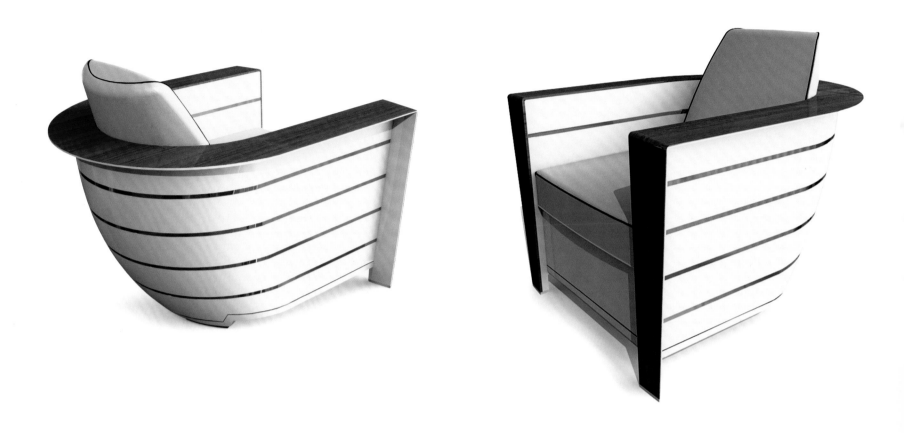

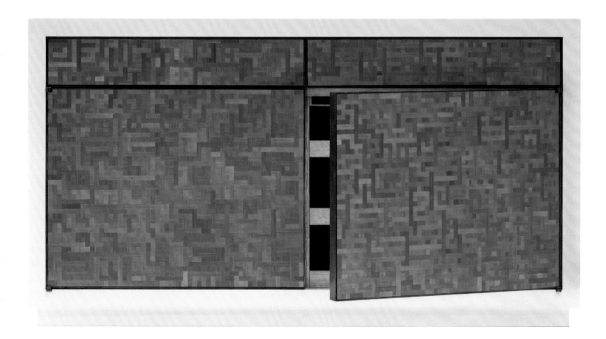

[opposite and left]
A white lacquer cabinet designed
by Photis Photi for Gosling for
a super-yacht in collaboration with
Todhunter Earle. The inset azure
panels are of geometric-cut
straw-work edged in bronze.

[above]
It was only the use of carbon fibre and
polished marine-grade steel that made
the creation of these tub chairs, based
on those of a 1930s ocean liner,
technically possible. The back of each
chair is formed from a series of
compound curves, allowing the chair to
fold into the base from different angles.
Straight stainless-steel lines serve to
add a sense of visual harmony and to
accentuate the sweep of the chair backs.

Selected Bibliography

Adam, Robert and James, *The Works in Architecture of Robert & James Adam*, New York and London, 1980

Benton, Charlotte, Tim Benton, Ghislaine Wood (eds), *Art Deco 1910–1939*, London and Boston, 2003

Britton, John, *The Union of Architecture, Sculpture and Painting*, London, 1827

Calloway, Stephen, *The Elements of Style*, new edn, London, 2005

Duncan, Alastair, *Art Deco Furniture*, new edn, London, 1992

Edwards, Clive, et al., *British Furniture 1600–2000*, London, 2005

Goff, Moira, et al., *Georgians Revealed: Life, Style and the Making of Modern Britain*, London, 2013

Marsden, Jonathan (ed.), *Victoria & Albert: Art & Love*, London, 2010

Morley, John, *Regency Design, 1790–1840*, London and New York, 1993

Olivier-Vial, Franck and François Rateau, *Armand Albert Rateau*, Paris, 1992

Saumarez Smith, Charles, *Eighteenth-Century Decoration: Design and the Domestic Interior in England*, London and New York, 1993

Snodin, Michael (ed.), *Horace Walpole's Strawberry Hill*, New Haven and London, 2009

Weber, Susan (ed.), *William Kent: Designing Georgian Britain*, New Haven and London, 2013

Picture Credits

Acknowledgments

I would particularly like to thank the following for their assistance: Neale Albert, Deborah Bennett, Leonora Birt, Paula Cairey, Helen Chislett, Jonathon Coleman, Kathleen Douglas, Jane Dundas, Lucie Kitchener, Lucinda Magraw, Michael Palin, Sarah Paynter, Sarah Ritchie, Chris and Suzanne Sharp, Isambard Thomas, Marianne Topham, Tim Walshe, and the team at Thames & Hudson (Jamie Camplin, Julian Honer, Julia MacKenzie and Maria Ranauro).

I am indebted to the extraordinary patience and talent of Stephen Calloway in making sense of the history and context of this book and my work.

I am also extremely grateful to all the many wonderful clients who have kindly allowed me to photograph both their furniture and their homes: and my sincere thanks to Lord Browne and Nghi Nguyen for their continued patronage, vision and imagination.

Great thanks also go to Jean Gomm for all her amazing foresight and immaculate planning.

I wish to express my gratitude to the following designers, architects and craftsmen for their contribution to the projects illustrated in this book.

GOSLING DESIGN TEAM
Ruby Mogford, Photis Photi, Phil Sturdy

DESIGNERS & ARCHITECTS
Ian Adam-Smith and James Raw at
Ian Adam-Smith Architects
www.ianadam-smith.co.uk

Chancery St James Designs

Lavinia Dargie at Dargie Lewis Designs
www.dargielewis.com

Jim Dunn at James Dunn Consulting
jamesdunnconsulting.co.uk

Victoria Fairfax
victoriafairfaxinteriors.com

Kelly Hoppen
kellyhoppeninteriors.com

Adam Hunter at Finchatton
www.finchatton.com

Rebecca Korner at Korner Interiors
www.kornerinteriors.com

David Linley
www.davidlinley.com

Judy Longbrook at JS Designs
www.jsdesigns-interiors.com

Patti Money-Coutts at Overbury Designs
www.overburydesigns.co.uk

Racheline Nahon at Lyndhurst Interiors

Anna Owens at Anna Owens Designs
www.annaowensdesigns.com

Lindy Thomas
www.lindythomasinteriors.com

Emily Todhunter and Kate Earle at Todhunter Earle
www.todhunterearle.com

Alberto Torsello and Barbara De Stefano
www.taarchitettura.com

Justin Van Breda
www.j-v-b.com

Joanna Wood
www.joannatrading.com

CRAFTSMEN
Karl Allan, Paul Barbier, Rupert Bevan, Sam Bouvet, Trevor Bradley, Heath Chadwick, Valentina Chirici, Jonathon Coleman, William Cowley, Angela Deacon, Mark Done, Alan Earl, Alan Englefield, Elaine Gardner; Adam Gilchrist at Veedon Fleece, Mikey Garbutt, Peter Gorman, Vivienne Griffin, Ian Haycock, Steve Holmes, Alex Hopper, Mike Horness, Yann and Sandra Jallu, Tom Jenkinson, Steve Keeling, Robert Kell, Florian Krenn, Ben Lemarie, Gareth Locker, Dmitri Liventsov, Bogdan Lurka, Chris Manship, Vitaly Moiseev, Luke Newland, Christine Palmer, Jack Pearson, Pitti Mosaici, John Robinson, Mark Robinson, Peter Rackstraw, Paul Reed, Gavin Rookledge, Nicolò Rubelli, Sam Turner, Sholeh Tavakoli, Allan Thompson, Yvonne Thompson, Richard Townsend, Mark Whiteley, Drew Whitemore.

In memory of Claire Englefield from Ace Marquetry.

Index

Page numbers in *italic* refer to illustrations